York Notes Rapid Revision

The Sign of the Four

AQA GCSE English Literature

Written by Maria Cairney

Pearson

YORK PRESS

YORK PRESS
322 Old Brompton Road, London SW5 9JH

PEARSON EDUCATION LIMITED
80 Strand, London, WC2R 0RL

© Librairie du Liban *Publishers* 2019

10 9 8 7 6 5 4 3 2 1

ISBN 978–1–2922–7096-8

Phototypeset by Ken Vail Graphic Design
Printed in Slovakia

Photo credits:
Everett Historical/Shutterstock for page 4 top / Leon Rafael/Shutterstock for page 6
top / Robin Weaver/Alamy for page 8 middle / ewaplesna/Shutterstock for page 10
middle / Martin Christopher Parker/Shutterstock for page 12 middle / Andrew Barnes/
Alamy for page 14 middle / Lotus_studio/Shutterstock for page 16 middle / ROBERTO
ZILLI/Shutterstock for page 18 middle / Karissaa/Shutterstock for page 20 middle /
Julia700702/Shutterstock for page 24 middle / Q44/Alamy for page 26 middle / Amoret
Tanner/Alamy for page 26 bottom / Mike Goldwater/Alamy for page 28 middle / J
Walters/Shutterstock for page 30 top / United Archives GmbH/Alamy for page 32 top
and 60 top / Serg Zastavkin/Shutterstock for page 34 top / Dmytro Spivak/Shutterstock
for page 36 top and 52 bottom / Ysbrand Cosijn/Shutterstock for page 38 top / henk
ten napel/Shutterstock for page 40 top / Dmytro Spivak/Shutterstock for 42 top and
bottom / mgkava/© iStock for page 46 bottom / AVN Photo Lab/Shutterstock for page
48 middle / LiliGraphie/© iStock for page 50 bottom / blickwinkel/Alamy for page 54
middle / fotorawin/Shutterstock for page 58 middle / Jeff Morgan 04/Alamy for page 60
bottom

CONTENTS

Three key things about Arthur Conan Doyle

1. Arthur Conan Doyle (1859–1930) was one of the most successful and popular writers of the Victorian and Edwardian eras.

2. He trained as a doctor at Edinburgh University and, while working as a GP, began writing stories, articles and even **novels** in his spare time.

3. His experiences as a student and assistant of Dr Joseph Bell in Edinburgh are said to have inspired his most famous creation, the **'unofficial consulting detective'** Sherlock Holmes.

How did the Sherlock Holmes stories begin?

- The first Holmes story, *A Study in Scarlet*, appeared in *Beeton's Christmas Annual* (1887).

- This was followed by *The Sign of the Four* (1890).

- The following year, when Conan Doyle was now working as an eye specialist in London's prestigious Harley Street, he began what became his most successful publishing partnership with *The Strand*, a popular and well-established monthly magazine.

How did readers respond to the Holmes stories?

- The style of the Holmes and Watson stories, with the duo tackling a new case each time, was perfect for the readers of *The Strand*. The adventures were a great success, and more Holmes stories followed until Conan Doyle decided to 'kill off' his creation in December 1893.

- Holmes had taken over his life, leaving him little time for anything else!

- In 1901, his famous detective was brought back from the dead to investigate 'The Hound of the Baskervilles', much to the delight of readers.

- Conan Doyle continued to publish new Holmes stories until the 1920s.

- He was awarded a knighthood in 1902 and continued writing medical tales, mysteries and adventures until his death in 1930.

Chapters 1 and 2

Sherlock Holmes is restless, waiting for the next case. He and his partner, Dr Watson, argue over Holmes's drug use and discuss the science of deduction. Miss Mary Morstan arrives unexpectedly at Baker Street. Dr Watson is struck both by Mary herself and her tragic circumstances. She is an orphan and her father, Captain Morstan, disappeared mysteriously ten years ago on returning from India. Mary has received annual gifts of pearls and now an anonymous letter requesting a night-time meeting.

Chapters 3–5

Holmes and Watson meet Miss Morstan who shows them a document which has 'the sign of the four'. They are taken across London to meet Thaddeus Sholto and then to Pondicherry Lodge, the home of his twin brother, Bartholomew Sholto. It seems the twins' deceased father, Major Sholto, and Captain Morstan obtained a fortune from India: the Agra treasure. Morstan, they learn, died accidentally during an argument over the fortune. At Pondicherry Lodge they discover the dead Bartholomew – murdered by a poisoned dart. The treasure is missing.

Chapters 10–12

A night-time river chase results in the capture of the wooden-legged man, Jonathan Small, and the death of his accomplice, the Andaman Islander, Tonga. When the treasure is lost forever, the news does not distress Miss Morstan because the barrier between her and Watson is now removed. Finally, Small relates his strange life story – involving the Indian Mutiny, the theft of the Agra treasure and tale of 'the four'. Watson tells Holmes of his engagement to Mary, but Holmes is unaffected by this news and begins the wait for his next case.

Chapters 6–9

Holmes and Watson begin the hunt for the killers – a wooden-legged man and his bare-foot accomplice. During the investigation the detective, Athelney Jones, wrongly arrests Thaddeus, but later Holmes and the police join forces. Watson's feelings for Miss Morstan grow, but he considers the treasure to be a barrier to their relationship.

PLOT AND STRUCTURE Chapters 1 and 2

Five key things about Chapters 1 and 2

1. We meet **Sherlock Holmes** – the world's **'only unofficial consulting detective'** – and find out about his **unusual methods** and his **character**.
2. **Dr Watson**, an injured war veteran and **Holmes's companion**, is presented as the **story's narrator**.
3. We see that **Holmes and Watson respect each other** but are very different characters; **Holmes** is only **interested in facts** while **Watson** is **more emotional**.
4. **Miss Morstan** is introduced and she **outlines her case** which **forms the plot** of the **novel**.
5. Several key **themes**, such as **love and friendship** and the **role of the British Empire** in the story, are indicated.

What happens in Chapter 1?

- The story begins one afternoon in Holmes's lodgings in London.
- Watson describes Holmes as he prepares to inject himself with a syringe of cocaine. They disagree about the risks of his drug use.
- Holmes provides Watson with an explanation of the **'exact science'** of detection.
- Holmes demonstrates his **'peculiar powers'** by precisely identifying Watson's movements that morning and describing Watson's brother, the owner of a pocket-watch, with pinpoint accuracy.
- Holmes is bored and looks out of the window at the **'dreary'** view, but his mood brightens with the sudden arrival of a new client, Miss Mary Morstan.

What happens in Chapter 2?

- Watson describes Miss Morstan. He notices her calm manner and the simplicity of her clothes which show she is not wealthy.
- Mary outlines her **'singular'** case: the disappearance of her father, the six anonymous gifts of a single pearl and now a mysterious letter. The men agree to go with her to the night-time meeting.
- Watson puts a stop to any **'dangerous thoughts'** about romance with Miss Morstan by reflecting upon his war injury and his own lack of money.

Five key quotations

1. Holmes sets the **tone** for a **crime story**: 'Detection is, or ought to be, an exact science, and should be treated in the same cold and unemotional manner.' (Chapter 1)

2. Watson introduces the theme of wealth in describing Miss Morstan: 'a plainness and simplicity about her costume … bore with it a suggestion of limited means' (Chapter 2)

3. Miss Morstan reveals a connection to the British Empire: 'a considerable number of curiosities from the Andaman Islands' (Chapter 2)

4. Holmes describes his scientific approach: 'A client is to me a mere unit,–a factor in a problem.' (Chapter 2)

5. Watson describes his social position: 'What was I, an army surgeon with a weak leg and a weaker banking-account …?'

Note it!

Conan Doyle's mysterious description of London with its swirling **'yellow fog'** matches other eerie, **Gothic settings** such as Pondicherry Lodge (in Chapter 5) and Jonathan Small's tale about Agra (Chapter 12).

Exam focus

How can I write about form? (AO2)

You can use Chapter 1 to write about the form of the story.

The opening chapter helps readers understand the type of story to expect. Holmes explains, 'Detection is, or ought to be, an exact science', setting this up as a crime story where 'exact' scientific methods will play an important part. Holmes's discussion of his scientific research also shows this. Finally, his careful study of Watson's watch highlights how precise analysis will eventually solve the mystery.	Topic sentence
	Relevant quotation to support introduction
	Term relating to form
	Detailed example to develop point

Now you try!

Finish this paragraph about introducing characters. Use one of the quotations from the list.

The opening chapter introduces Holmes, and the reader's first impression is that ....

PLOT AND STRUCTURE Chapters 3 and 4

Five key things about Chapters 3 and 4

1. The **themes** of **justice and wealth** become important and 'the Sign of the Four' is first mentioned.
2. The night-time ride across **London** features **atmospheric descriptions of setting** which build tension and **suspense**.
3. We are introduced to the **characters** of **Thaddeus** and **Bartholomew Sholto** and hear of their father, **Major Sholto**.
4. We learn about **Captain Morstan's death** and the **lost Agra treasure**.
5. Thaddeus explains the **mystery of the pearls**.

What happens in Chapter 3?

- Holmes discovers the **'suggestive fact'** that Miss Morstan was first contacted after Major Sholto's death. Holmes states this case must involve the Sholto heirs and their need to offer **'compensation'**.
- On the way to the theatre meeting Mary reveals her father's document showing a diagram of a building and a strange **symbol** – **'sign of the four,**
  – Jonathan Small, Mahomet Singh, Abdullah Khan, Dost Akbar'.
- Watson notes the **'eerie'** and **'ghost-like'** images of London.
- A mysterious coachman takes them to a suburban house with a **'Hindoo servant'** wearing a yellow turban and white robes, contrasting sharply with the dark streets.

What happens in Chapter 4?

- The trio meet Thaddeus Sholto whose odd appearance and manner are matched only by the unusual style of his exotically furnished home.
- Thaddeus, after asking Dr Watson to examine his heart, reveals to Miss Morstan that her father is dead. Then he tells of Major Sholto's disagreement with Morstan over the Agra treasure, Morstan's accidental death, and the Major's own shocking death from seeing the stranger with **'wild cruel eyes'**. He tells of the brothers' hunt for the lost treasure and their attempt to make amends to Miss Morstan with the pearls.
- The trio, with Thaddeus, leave for Pondicherry Lodge to meet his brother, Bartholomew, who has now discovered the lost treasure.

Five key quotations

1. Holmes describes the Sign of the Four symbol: 'a curious hieroglyphic like four crosses in a line with their arms touching' (Chapter 3)

2. Watson on London at night: 'the monster tentacles which the giant city was throwing out into the country' (Chapter 3)

3. The theme of wealth experienced by Major Sholto: 'The cursed greed which has been my besetting sin through life' (Chapter 4)

4. Elements of a **crime story**: 'a single footmark was visible' (Chapter 4)

5. Thaddeus about Bartholomew Sholto: 'my brother was himself a little inclined to my father's fault' (Chapter 4)

Note it!

Major Sholto returned from India with **'a considerable sum of money'** along with **'valuable curiosities'** and **'native servants'**. This shows how the British used colonial rule to become wealthy. Such greedy and oppressive behaviour fuelled the Indian revolt described by Jonathan Small in Chapter 12.

Exam focus

How can I write about language? AO2

You can use Chapter 3 to write about Conan Doyle's use of **personification**.

Chapter 3 is significant because it introduces the 'sign of the four' symbol. Conan Doyle describes it as a curious hieroglyphic and this phrase suggests the mystery will be like an ancient language which must be deciphered. Next the simile 'like four crosses in a line with their arms touching' uses personification to create a powerful image of the four men linked together forever by their actions.

| Topic sentence makes point |
| Relevant quotation |
| Detailed explanation |
| Use of literary terms to develop interpretation |

Now you try!

Finish this paragraph about setting. Use one of the quotations from the list.

In the mysterious London night-time setting, Conan Doyle describes the city as having ....

Five key things about Chapters 5 and 6

1. With the **discovery of the murder** of Bartholomew Sholto at Pondicherry Lodge, this now becomes a **crime story**.

2. **Dr Watson's and Miss Morstan's feelings deepen** as dark events draw them closer together.

3. We are given a demonstration of **Holmes's scientific methods** of detection.

4. The **close working relationship** between **Holmes and Watson** becomes clear.

5. The rash and arrogant police detective, **Athelney Jones**, is introduced.

What happens in Chapter 5?

- Holmes, Watson, Mary and Thaddeus Sholto arrive at Pondicherry Lodge, a gloomy building, which is carefully secured and guarded.

- Bartholomew has not been seen all day. The group discover his body in his laboratory, and are horrified by his **'ghastly, inscrutable smile'**.

- Dr Watson is baffled by events. In contrast to this, when Holmes discovers another 'sign of the four', the brown stick and the thorn behind Bartholomew's ear, he is confident they could have **'an entirely connected case'**.

- The treasure has been taken. Thaddeus, the last person to see his brother alive, selfishly worries himself into a **'frenzy'** that he will be blamed for the death, but Holmes calms him and sends him to fetch the police.

What happens in Chapter 6?

- Before the police arrive, Holmes provides Watson with a demonstration of his precise observations. He points to an impression of a wooden stump and states that the crime was committed by **'the wooden legged man'** and his mysterious ally who has left strange, small, naked footprints.

- Athelney Jones arrives and disagrees with Holmes. Jones wants to close his **'net'** on Thaddeus, whereas Holmes names Jonathan Small, the wooden-legged man, as one of the culprits.

- Watson escorts Mary home and Holmes instructs him to return with the tracker dog, Toby.

Five key quotations

1. The **setting** of Pondicherry Lodge: 'with its gloom and its deathly silence struck a chill to the heart' (Chapter 5)

2. Love between Watson and Mary: 'in an hour of trouble our hands instinctively sought for each other' (Chapter 5)

3. The friendship of Holmes and Watson: 'My dear Watson ... You know my methods. Apply them' (Chapter 6)

4. Watson using his scientific knowledge: 'Death from some powerful vegetable alkaloid' (Chapter 6)

5. The **character** of Athelney Jones: 'Stern facts here,– no room for theories.' (Chapter 6)

Note it!

Holmes's entry to Pondicherry Lodge is made easier because he knows the **'prize fighter'** guarding it. The fact that Holmes appears to have once been a well-known amateur boxer reveals more about his life in the underworld of drugs (Chapter 1) and petty criminals (Chapter 8).

Exam focus

How can I write about the role of Jones? AO1

You can write about the arrogance of Athelney Jones.

With the introduction of Athelney Jones, there is almost immediately a disagreement between the detective and Holmes. Jones says he has 'no room for theories' and dismisses Holmes's entire approach to detection where scientific 'theories' are precisely applied. This not only shows how over-confident and arrogant Jones's character is, but also sets up wider conflict between the police and Holmes which develops as the story progresses.

Annotation
Topic sentence makes point
Relevant quotation
Detailed explanation
Further points about character

Now you try!

Finish this paragraph about the theme of friendship. Use one of the quotations from the list.

The theme of friendship is explored in Chapter 6 through the close working relationship between ....

Five key things about Chapters 7-9

1. Watson **recaps events** so far.
2. There are **comic moments** as the tracker dog, Toby, follows the wrong scent and later Holmes's old-man disguise fools both Watson and Jones.
3. The **characters** of **Mordecai Smith** and the **Baker Street Irregulars** are introduced as the investigation moves to the River Thames.
4. Holmes explains how he identified **Jonathan Small** as the wooden-legged man and, later, why he believes Small's companion is an **Andaman Islander**.
5. **Holmes announces a breakthrough** and Jones follows his lead.

What happens in Chapter 7?

- Watson escorts Mary home, then collects Toby from Mr Sherman's house with its **'queer animal family'**.
- Holmes, Watson and Toby now follow the trail from Pondicherry Lodge back into London while Holmes explains Jonathan Small's likely motive: **'having his revenge upon the man who had wronged him'**.
- Holmes and Watson laugh after Toby has taken them the wrong way.

What happens in Chapter 8?

- Back on the **'true scent'**, both men arrive at Mordecai Smith's wharf.
- Holmes calls upon his **'unofficial force,—the Baker Street irregulars'** to help him locate Smith's steam launch, the *Aurora*, on which Smith, Small and his Islander accomplice have escaped.
- Meanwhile, Holmes learns from a newspaper report of Thaddeus's arrest on suspicion of Bartholomew's murder.

What happens in Chapter 9?

- Nearly two days pass with no news from the Irregulars. Holmes becomes increasingly restless and decides to set out alone to find the men.
- A newspaper reports that Thaddeus has been released without charge. Both Jones and Watson are fooled by the arrival of the aged **'seafaring'** man – Holmes in disguise.

Five key quotations

1. Mrs Forrester's house: 'a tranquil English home in the midst of the wild, dark business which had absorbed us' (Chapter 7)

2. Holmes on the **theme** of justice: 'it was not a common murder but, … something in the nature of an act of justice' (Chapter 7)

3. Watson on the theme of love: 'if I found [the treasure] it would probably put her forever beyond my reach' (Chapter 8)

4. Holmes about the Irregulars: 'They can go everywhere, see everything, overhear everyone.' (Chapter 8)

5. Athelney Jones's change of attitude: 'His expression was downcast, and his bearing meek and even apologetic.' (Chapter 9)

Note it!

In Chapter 9, when the investigation stalls, Watson begins to question Holmes's theories about the case. This is the first time we see Watson doubt his friend as, in previous chapters, he has been happy to play the role of pupil with Holmes as expert teacher.

Exam focus

How can I write about the theme of love? AO1

You can use Chapter 8 to explore the theme of love.

> The theme of love is explored here through Watson's feelings for Miss Morstan. The reader realises Watson's dilemma when he says finding the treasure will 'probably put her forever beyond my reach'. Watson, however, is still determined to help recover the treasure even though Mary's gain will 'probably' result in his loss. Conan Doyle subtly implies that loving relationships are built upon such selfless acts.

- Clear topic sentence
- Relevant quotation explores idea
- Detailed explanation
- Further development of point

Now you try!

Finish this paragraph about settings. Use one of the quotations from the list.

In Chapter 7 there is a contrast between different settings with Watson's description of the house of ....

Five key things about Chapter 10

1. We learn more about **Holmes's character** and **his philosophy**.
2. The **night-time river chase** reaches a **dramatic climax**. Holmes and the police work together to catch the criminals.
3. **Mordecai Smith, Jonathan Small** and the **Islander** are described.
4. Although the treasure box is recovered and the criminals caught, **the Islander's death** during the chase raises questions about **crime** and **justice**.
5. The language used to describe the Islander reflects **Victorian attitudes** and the **context** of the **British Empire**.

What happens at the start of Chapter 10?

- After sharing dinner, Holmes, Watson and Jones head for Westminster Wharf to board a fast police-boat. Holmes asks Watson to bring his army revolver.

- While lying in wait for Small, Holmes explains how he discovered the *Aurora* in Jacobson's boat-yard and how his disguise enabled him to overhear Mordecai Smith's plans.

- Jones at first disagrees with Holmes's risky approach to the hunt, but is then persuaded by Holmes that he has **'thought over every possible course, and this is the best'**.

What happens during the chase?

- The *Aurora* appears and the chase begins. A slow tugboat blocks the police-boat's way and Holmes fears they have lost the chase. Only with the **'fierce energy'** of its frantically overloaded boilers do they recover lost ground.

- The crew of the *Aurora* is now visible; Small is **'cursing'** while the Islander, a **'savage, distorted creature'**, raises a blowpipe to his lips.

- Holmes and Watson fire their revolvers at the Islander. The boat runs aground. Small tries to escape, but is caught when his wooden leg sinks in the mud.

- While the treasure is found, there is no trace of the Islander. A **'murderous dart'** in the police-boat reveals the **'horrible death'** they have avoided.

Five key quotations

1. Holmes's change of mood: 'His bright humour marked the reaction from his black depression of the preceding days.'
2. Holmes describing Mordecai's wealth: 'he was very flush of money, chucking shillings about to the men'
3. Holmes about science: 'Individuals vary, but percentages remain constant. So says the statistician.'
4. **Form** of **crime story**: 'never did sport give me such a wild thrill as this mad, flying man-hunt down the Thames'
5. The **theme** of crime and justice: 'Never have I seen features so deeply marked with all bestiality and cruelty.'

Note it!

Conan Doyle's dramatic description of the river chase and the Islander's death uses powerful **onomatopoeic verbs** and **images** of dark and light to add tension. Similar effects are seen in Jonathan Small's account of the murder of the merchant Achmet at Agra (Chapter 12).

Exam focus

How can I write about the theme of crime and justice?

You can use Chapter 10 to write about the theme of justice.

> The death of the Islander who murdered Bartholomew Sholto raises the question of justice. The reader may think that justice has been done because Watson says the Islander's face was 'deeply marked with bestiality and cruelty.' While these nouns are associated with violent, animalistic behaviour, the reader might later question whether the killing was fair as Small suggests he was acting as his devoted and loyal servant.

- Point on specific theme
- Relevant supporting quotation
- Analysis of language
- Further development of point

Now you try!

Finish this paragraph about the form of the crime story. Use one of the quotations from the list.

The crime story form is apparent when Watson says that ....

PLOT AND STRUCTURE Chapter 11

Five key things about Chapter 11

1. We learn in **detail** what happened on the night of the **murder of Bartholomew Sholto** at Pondicherry Lodge.

2. The arrogant **character** of **Athelney Jones** is **contrasted** with that of **Watson** who, unlike Jones, is generous to others and humble about his own achievements.

3. **Watson's idealised description** of Mary's angelic appearance reveals much about **Victorian attitudes to women**.

4. When **Watson and Mary** meet, it becomes clear that both are reluctant to open the **treasure box** because of how it will affect their relationship.

5. The **theme** of **wealth** is explored when **Watson's declaration of love** is made only after Mary's chance of a fortune has been removed.

What happens at the start of Chapter 11?

- Jonathan Small, now a prisoner, reveals to Holmes that he never intended to kill Bartholomew Sholto and that it was entirely the fault of the **'little devil'**, Tonga.

- Small reflects upon the curse of the Agra treasure which has brought misery to all.

- Athelney Jones arrives and immediately tries to take full credit for the night's events. However, he honours his agreement to let Watson open the box with Mary.

What happens when the box is opened?

- Watson takes the treasure box to Mary's lodgings where he reflects upon the beauty of her **'sweet grave face'**.

- During his account to Mary of the chase for the treasure, Watson is quick to praise the **'analytical genius'** of his friend Sherlock Holmes.

- Mary is mainly concerned about the **'horrible peril'** the men have endured as Watson notes there is no **'eagerness in her voice'** to discuss the treasure.

- The iron box is forced open. It is heavy only because of its thick metal construction and is, in fact, empty.

- Watson is delighted that the **'golden barrier'** of wealth has come down and he can admit his feelings to Mary. The couple embrace.

Five key quotations

1. Small reflects views about the colonies: 'that little hell-hound Tonga who shot one of his cursed darts'

2. Jones's character: 'Jones was already beginning to give himself airs'

3. Small on the theme of wealth: 'it brought murder, to Major Sholto it brought fear and guilt, to me it has meant slavery for life'

4. Theme of Victorian attitudes to women: 'she was ... dressed in some sort of white diaphanous material, with a little touch of scarlet at the neck and waist'

5. The theme of love: 'Whoever had lost a treasure, I knew that night that I had gained one.'

Note it!

In Chapter 11, Watson's selfless praise for Holmes reflects the strength of the two men's friendship. This is mirrored in the final chapter when Jonathan Small tells of his absolute loyalty to the others who formed **'the sign of the four'**.

Exam focus

How can I write about context?

You can explore the context of colonialism through Small's account.

> The colonial context is evident here in Jonathan Small's comments about Tonga. He calls Tonga a 'little hell-hound', a description that makes him seem like an evil animal. This is developed when Small mentions Tonga's 'cursed darts' where the adjective 'cursed' also suggests magic. Similar language is used in Watson's earlier description of Tonga's appearance and reflects Victorian attitudes that colonised peoples were uncivilised, even less than human.

Clear topic sentence

Relevant quotation explores idea

Additional analysis

Analysis completed

Now you try!

Finish this paragraph about how love is presented. Use one of the quotations from the list.

The theme of love is apparent when Watson states ....

Five key things about Chapter 12

1. We learn that the **treasure is now lost forever**.

2. The significance of the **Sign of the Four** is finally revealed in Jonathan Small's detailed account of his time in India along with important **context** about **British colonialism**.

3. The behaviour of **Major Sholto**, with his **greed** and **betrayal** of others, is **contrasted** with that of **Tonga** whose **loyalty** to Small is absolute.

4. The **themes** of **crime and justice**, **love and friendship** and **wealth** become particularly significant in the final chapter.

5. Although both the crime and the true criminals may be unclear, Watson's announcement of his engagement to Mary provides a **decisive conclusion**.

What happens at the start of Chapter 12?

- Back at Baker Street, Small tells Holmes, Watson and Jones that the treasure is scattered for miles along the Thames riverbed.

- Small snarls at Jones's mention of **'justice'** and then tells his own story of suffering with **'fury'** and **'passion'**.

- He describes the loss of his leg in a crocodile attack and the events of the Indian Mutiny. He explains how he joined Singh and Khan at Agra and how, with Akbar, they stole the treasure and swore an oath to the Sign of the Four.

- Small then describes the brutal murder of the merchant Achmet which led to the Four's imprisonment in the Andaman Islands while the treasure lay undiscovered at Agra.

- Finally, Small tells of Sholto's betrayal, his escape from the Andamans and Bartholomew's death at the hands of his **'faithful mate'**, Tonga.

How does the story conclude?

- As Small is taken into custody, Watson ends the **'little drama'** by announcing his engagement to Mary Morstan.

- Holmes first gives a **'dismal groan'** at the news, but then praises Watson's choice of wife.

- The final image is of Holmes reaching for **'the cocaine-bottle'**.

Five key quotations

1. Small on the theme of justice: 'Whose loot is this, if it is not ours?'

2. Small's view of British India: 'these men that we fought against ... were our own picked troops'

3. Khan on the pursuit of wealth: 'We only ask you to do that which your countrymen come to this land for. We ask you to be rich.'

4. Khan's story within the novel: 'Hearken, then, to what I have to say.'

5. Holmes's **character**: 'But love is an emotional thing, and ... is opposed to that true cold reason which I place above all things.'

Note it!

There are several examples of how wealth corrupts. Khan condemns the rajah for hoarding his treasure and betraying India by supporting both sides in the Mutiny. Similarly, when Major Sholto obtains the treasure, he betrays Morstan and the Four by refusing to divide it.

Exam focus

How can I write about the theme of justice? (AO1)

You can use some of Small's views to explore the theme of justice.

Conan Doyle explores the theme of justice through Small's question in the final chapter when he asks 'Whose loot is this, if it is not ours?' It is a rhetorical question which the reader is then forced to consider. The use of the word 'loot', meaning stolen items, highlights the final justice of the treasure being lost forever as none of the characters ever had any real right to this wealth.

— Clear topic sentence with quotation

— Analysis with correct term

— Additional analysis

— Concluding point

Now you try!

Finish this paragraph about structure. Use one of the quotations from the list.

The structure of the novel includes other stories: for example, when Abdullah Khan invites the reader ....

My progress   Needs more work ☐   Getting there ☐   Sorted! ☐

Five key things about form and structure

1. The **novel** is narrated in the **first person** by Dr Watson as a **frame narrator**.

2. The events of the novel appear in **chronological order**, but **characters** do refer to earlier events in **flashbacks**.

3. There are **stories within stories** in the novel and Watson relates them all.

4. Although the genre is a **detective story** – with a crime to be solved – the narrative has **Gothic** elements and a **romantic subplot** between Dr Watson and Miss Morstan.

5. The main **plot** is **action-driven**, rather than **character-driven** – the **climax** of the main action plot is therefore the river chase.

Why is the narrative structure important?

- We view all events through Watson's eyes so Mary is always presented romantically and Holmes remains mysterious.

- The timeline of the main story runs across just four days and nights; this maintains the fast **pace** of the action, but the flashbacks allow for the full story to be revealed as we go along.

- Dr Watson is a trustworthy guide: the reader must rely on his account of Mary's story, Thaddeus's re-telling of Major Sholto's story and Jonathan Small's **'strange story'** which includes Abdullah Khan's tale.

How does the detective form work?

- The detective genre creates **suspense**, but the Gothic episodes generate fear: the romantic subplot provides a lighter, more positive narrative **counterpoint** to these.

- The events of the case reveal details about Holmes's character, but the only character who really develops in the story is Dr Watson through his relationship with Mary.

- If the three main parts of this story are the problem (the presentation of Mary's case), the climax (the river chase) and the **resolution** (Jonathan Small's capture), Chapter 12 – 'The strange story of Jonathan Small' – can be seen either as an **anti-climax** or an extended resolution to the story.

Five key quotations

1. Watson as narrator: 'a small brochure with the somewhat fantastic title of "A Study in Scarlet"'

2. Jonathan Small's story: '[my family] were all steady, chapel-going folk, small farmers ... I was always a bit of a rover'

3. Thaddeus Sholto's story: 'I must prepare you by showing you how we all stand to each other ... I can only lay the facts before you as I know them myself.'

4. Discovery of the murder: 'Moonlight was streaming into the room ... and suspended ... in the air, for all beneath was in shadow, there hung a face'

5. Watson: 'This is all an insoluble mystery to me ... It grows darker instead of clearer.'

Note it!

Conan Doyle pauses the action so that readers can catch up on events. Holmes and Watson go over the case before and during their night-time walk into London (Chapters 6 and 7) and two newspaper reports (Chapters 8 and 9) provide the police perspective on the case.

Exam focus

How can I write about form and structure? AO2

You can use Dr Watson's narration to explore the novel's form and structure.

Dr Watson, as the frame narrator, is the reader's guide to the mysterious events. Conan Doyle shows that Dr Watson is as confused as the reader when he calls the case a mystery that 'grows darker instead of clearer'. This sets up an expectation that, as a detective story, the mystery will eventually be solved and Holmes's powers will throw light on any 'darkness'.

- Focus on structure
- Relevant support
- Reference to form
- Further analysis

Now you try!

Finish this paragraph about form. Use one of the quotations from the list.

Gothic elements, which heighten tension, are revealed in the description of the discovery ....

1. Look at this ideas map representing the **plot** and structure of Chapters 1 and 2. Is there anything else you could add?

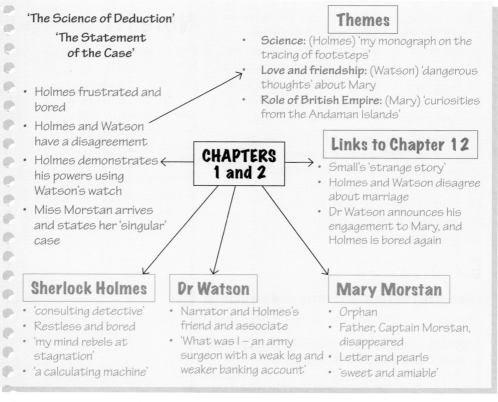

'The Science of Deduction'

'The Statement of the Case'

- Holmes frustrated and bored
- Holmes and Watson have a disagreement
- Holmes demonstrates his powers using Watson's watch
- Miss Morstan arrives and states her 'singular' case

Themes

- Science: (Holmes) 'my monograph on the tracing of footsteps'
- Love and friendship: (Watson) 'dangerous thoughts' about Mary
- Role of British Empire: (Mary) 'curiosities from the Andaman Islands'

CHAPTERS 1 and 2

Links to Chapter 12

- Small's 'strange story'
- Holmes and Watson disagree about marriage
- Dr Watson announces his engagement to Mary, and Holmes is bored again

Sherlock Holmes

- 'consulting detective'
- Restless and bored
- 'my mind rebels at stagnation'
- 'a calculating machine'

Dr Watson

- Narrator and Holmes's friend and associate
- 'What was I – an army surgeon with a weak leg and weaker banking account'

Mary Morstan

- Orphan
- Father, Captain Morstan, disappeared
- Letter and pearls
- 'sweet and amiable'

2. Create your own ideas map for one of the other chapters.

Quick quiz

Answer these quick questions about the plot and structure of the novel:

1. In Chapter 1 who does Holmes 'deduce' was the original owner of Watson's watch?
2. In Chapter 2 how many pearls does Mary say were sent to her in total? How often?
3. In Chapter 3 what sign is on the curious paper that belonged to Mary's father?
4. What is unusual about the servant who opens the door in the suburban house in Chapter 3?

5. In Chapter 4 what does Thaddeus Sholto first ask Dr Watson?

6. Where do the group travel next at the end of Chapter 4?

7. What objects are found on and near Bartholomew's body in Chapter 5?

8. What does Thaddeus fear will happen to him?

9. What unusual mark does Holmes discover beside the naked foot mark in Chapter 6?

10. In Chapter 6 who comes to help with the case?

11. Who helps Holmes and Watson track the criminals in Chapter 7?

12. What is the name of the group that Holmes recruits in Chapter 8?

13. Whose release from custody is reported in the newspaper in Chapter 9?

14. What is the name of the boat-yard where the *Aurora* is discovered in Chapter 10?

15. What happens to prevent Jonathan Small from escaping at the end of Chapter 10?

16. What do Watson and Mary discover about the iron box in Chapter 11?

17. How does Watson react to the news about the treasure in Chapter 11?

18. What uprising does Small describe in Chapter 12?

19. Who is the merchant whose murder is described in Chapter 12?

20. What announcement provides a happy conclusion to the novel?

Power paragraphs

Write a paragraph in response to **each of these questions**. For each, try to **use one quotation** you have learned from this section.

1. How is the character of Holmes presented in Chapter 1?

2. How does Dr Watson react to the loss of the Agra treasure?

Exam practice

Re-read the section in Chapter 1 from 'Now, I have here a watch' to 'more faith in your marvellous faculty' where Watson asks Holmes to examine his watch.

What does this episode reveal about Holmes and Watson? Write **two paragraphs** explaining your ideas. You could comment on:

● Holmes's methods of deduction

● how Watson reacts to Holmes's findings.

SETTING AND CONTEXT Victorian Britain

Five key things about Victorian Britain

1. During the reign of Queen Victoria (1837–1901) there was a **strong divide between the different classes**. Although free education was more accessible, there was still **little social mobility**.
2. **Women** did not have the vote and were often **limited to domestic roles**. Homemaking was seen as the most suitable occupation for middle-class women or **'angels of the house'**.
3. **Non-white races** were viewed with suspicion and fear. White European culture was considered to be 'civilised' while **other cultures were viewed as inferior** or even 'savage'.
4. The **Metropolitan Police Force** was established in response to fears about rising crime in London. The death penalty was enforced and convict colonies, such as the **Andaman Islands**, were used for overseas prisoners.
5. The **Victorian age** was one of **scientific discovery**; by the 1890s, belief in organised religion had declined and many people turned to science for solutions to society's problems.

Where are these issues explored?

- Mr Sherman (Chapter 7), the Smiths (Chapter 8) and the Baker Street Irregulars (Chapter 8) are all examples of lower-class **characters** in the **novel**.
- Watson's descriptions of **'sweet and amiable'** Mary reflect Victorian attitudes to women: her beauty (Chapters 2 and 11) and her caring nature are emphasised (Chapter 5).
- The Islander is initially presented as much more dangerous and wild than his white associate, Small (Chapter 10).

Where is social change revealed?

- Newspaper reports celebrate the **'prompt and energetic action'** of the police (Chapter 8) whereas Small's account of the Andaman Islands emphasises the severe punishment of criminals (Chapter 12).
- Holmes and Watson constantly use scientific language – Holmes conducts chemical analysis (Chapter 9) and Bartholomew's rooms in Pondicherry Lodge have a laboratory (Chapter 5).

Five key quotations

1. Holmes on the shipyard workers: 'Dirty-looking rascals, but I suppose every one has some little immortal spark concealed about him.'

2. Watson on Mary: 'The soft light of a shaded lamp fell upon her playing over her sweet, grave face and ... the rich coils of her luxuriant hair.'

3. Watson on Tonga: 'I whipped out [my pistol] at the sight of this savage, distorted creature.'

4. Small on the Andaman Islands: 'a dreary, fever-stricken place ... infested with wild cannibal natives'

5. Holmes's belief in science: 'Detection is, or ought to be, an exact science'

Note it!

Holmes's attitude to lower-class characters is often critical. He does not trust the Smiths, calling them **'people of that sort'** (Chapter 8) and cannot believe that Jonathan Small is capable of detailed planning because he lacks education (Chapter 10).

Exam focus

How can I write about the Victorian social context?

You can use descriptions of lower-class characters to explore context.

When Holmes and Watson are hiding in the shipyards in Chapter 10, Holmes notices the workers. Holmes calls them 'dirty-looking rascals', his use of the noun 'rascals' suggesting he views lower-class men as untrustworthy. He does admit that like 'every one' these men have souls or an 'immortal spark' but then adds 'I suppose'. This uncertain verb reflects middle-class Victorians' critical attitudes towards the lower classes.	Introduces specific example
	Relevant support with analysis of language
	Develops the point
	Link to context

Now you try!

Finish this paragraph about attitudes to race. Use one of the quotations from the list.

Victorian attitudes to race are reflected when Watson describes Tonga ....

My progress Needs more work ☐ Getting there ☐ Sorted! ☐

Five key things about colonialism and the British Empire

1. The main events of the **novel** take place in **London** and in **India**, at the time an important British colony.

2. By the end of the Victorian period in 1901, the **British Empire** included nearly a quarter of the world's population and was a major source of trade, resources and **wealth**.

3. The events of the **Indian Mutiny** (1857–8), a revolt of Indian soldiers against the British army, gives Conan Doyle the backdrop for the theft of the **Agra treasure**.

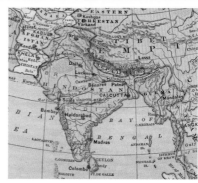

4. The British colony of the **Andaman Islands** in the Bay of Bengal was used to hold prisoners captured during the Indian Mutiny.

5. The **Victorian ruling classes** believed they were superior to the **colonised peoples** they governed; they were often dismissive of non-white races and cultures.

How is the wealth and drama of the British Empire represented?

- We learn that Major Sholto had retired from the Indian army and that he had **'prospered in India'** (Chapter 4).

- Thaddeus Sholto's house is full of exotic objects and artistic treasures which originated from countries across the British Empire (Chapter 4).

- Jonathan Small's account of the Indian Mutiny at the end of the novel is dramatic and engaging (Chapter 12).

How are colonised peoples represented?

- Major Sholto's response to the **'three black fellows'**, the non-white members of the Four (Chapter 12), and Watson's descriptions of the Islander Tonga (Chapter 10) reflect Victorian attitudes to colonised peoples or 'natives'.

- Despite Small's loyalty and friendship to Tonga, he exploits his **'faithful mate'** for money, exhibiting him like a kind of exotic animal.

Five key quotations

1. Thaddeus: '[Major Sholto] brought back ... a considerable sum of money, a large collection of valuable curiosities, and a staff of native servants.'

2. Major Sholto: 'What have three black fellows to do with our agreement?'

3. Jonathan Small on Tonga: 'He was devoted to me and would do anything to serve me'

4. The Indian Mutiny: 'The beating of drums, the rattle of tomtoms and the yells and howls of the rebels'

5. Small: 'We earned a living ... by my exhibiting poor Tonga at fairs ... as the black cannibal'

Note it!

Watson mentions that he suffered his war injury in the Afghan campaign (Chapter 1). In this colonial war the British army was safeguarding British territories around India. Symbolically, Watson fires his revolver from his military service against Tonga (Chapter 12).

Exam focus

How can I write about colonialism and empire? AO3

You can use the theme of wealth to explore this context.

Conan Doyle shows that Major Sholto's time in India brought him excessive wealth. Thaddeus says his father's list of rewards included 'a considerable sum of money' and 'a large collection of valuable curiosities'. The use of the adjectives 'considerable', 'large' and 'valuable' here emphasises just how much money was made by exploiting the resources of the countries in the British Empire.

- Introduces example linked to theme
- Relevant support
- Analysis of language
- Link to context

Now you try!

Finish this paragraph about Victorian attitudes to people from the British Empire. Use one of the quotations from the list.

Jonathan Small's praise for Tonga's sense of duty is shown by ....

Five key settings

1. The address of **221B Baker Street** is shared by Holmes and Watson, with the housekeeper Mrs Hudson, and provides the base for their investigation.

2. After the night-time meeting, Holmes, Watson and Mary are taken to **Thaddeus Sholto's house** in a **'questionable and forbidding neighborhood'** of London.

3. **Pondicherry Lodge** in Upper Norwood is six miles from the city and is a grand mansion owned by Major Sholto, now occupied by his son Bartholomew.

4. The Indian city of **Agra** is the **setting** for most of Jonathan Small's story; it is during the Indian Mutiny in this city that the treasure is stolen.

5. The **River Thames**, its shipyards and muddy riverbanks provide an atmospheric setting for the hunt and capture of the criminals.

How are the domestic settings significant?

- The Baker Street lodgings (Chapters 1 and 10) in the heart of London reflect the strong friendship between Holmes and Watson as well as their professional partnership.

- Thaddeus Sholto's house (Chapters 2 and 3) with its exotic furnishings and art objects, along with its Indian servants, reveals not only a fashionable interest in the 'East' but also the wealth of the British Empire.

- Pondicherry Lodge (Chapter 5) is isolated and heavily guarded – a mysterious **Gothic** setting for Bartholomew Sholto's murder.

- Mrs Forrester's house is a peaceful **'English home'**, providing a tranquil, domestic contrast to the dark, criminal events of the rest of the **novel** (Chapter 7).

What role do settings play in the action?

- The Indian city of Agra (Chapter 12), another mysterious and exotic setting, is at the centre of the Indian Mutiny and is important for understanding British imperial attitudes.

- The exciting night-time river chase and the capture of Small in the mudbanks of the Thames (Chapter 10) provide a dramatic and atmospheric **climax** to the **crime story**.

Five key quotations

1. Watson in Baker Street: 'Our meal was a merry one. Holmes could talk exceedingly well … I have never known him so brilliant.'
2. Thaddeus's home: 'Two great tiger-skins … increased the suggestion of Eastern luxury, as did a huge hookah which stood upon a mat'
3. Pondicherry Lodge: 'a gravel path wound … to a huge clump of a house … all plunged in shadow save where a moonbeam struck'
4. The old quarter in Agra: 'great deserted halls, and winding passages'
5. The Thames riverbank: 'It was a wild and desolate place, where the moon glimmered upon a wide expanse of marsh-land, with pools of stagnant water'

Quick quiz

Answer these quick questions about the setting and context of the novel:

1. What is the name given to the group of street children who help Holmes with his investigation?
2. Who is described as 'a savage, distorted creature'?
3. Whose 'prompt and energetic action' is praised in the newspaper report in Chapter 8?
4. Whose 'sweet and amiable' nature is praised by Dr Watson?
5. Where is Jonathan Small captured?
6. Which Indian city is the setting for most of Jonathan Small's story?
7. Where are the lodgings shared by Holmes and Watson?
8. Who is praised for his devotion and desire to serve?
9. Who brought back 'a large collection of valuable curiosities' from India?
10. What is the name of the uprising taking place when Small is in Agra?

Power paragraphs

Choose one **setting** or **context** related to the novel. Write **two paragraphs** explaining how Conan Doyle uses this setting or context in relation to either a) theme or b) character.

Five key things about Sherlock Holmes

1. **Holmes** is a new type of **Victorian investigator** who solves crimes using the **latest scientific techniques** and theories.

2. He has an **extensive knowledge of London** and its **criminal underworld**.

3. Due to his **incredible intelligence**, he can often appear **arrogant** and critical of others.

4. His manner is **detached** and **unemotional**.

5. He has **no close** associates or friends, **except Dr Watson**.

What do we learn about Holmes at the beginning of the novel?

- Holmes becomes frustrated when he is not working on a case, even going to the extremes of taking cocaine.

- He is the world's only **'unofficial consulting detective'**: a role which he himself has created.

- He enjoys demonstrating his skills of scientific observation and deduction.

- He is not motivated by fame and is therefore unimpressed by Dr Watson's pamphlet, *A Study in Scarlet*, about their previous case.

- He carries out scientific research and publishes academic papers on his methods.

How does Holmes's character develop?

- **Chapters 1 and 6:** Holmes leads by example demonstrating his powers of deduction to Dr Watson and others.

- **Chapter 8:** There are signs that he cares about Dr Watson, e.g. asking about his war-injured leg **(Chapter 7)** and even playing him to sleep with his violin.

- **Chapters 1 and 8:** He makes fun of Athelney Jones and the police saying that they are often **'out of their depths'**.

- **Chapters 1 and 9:** As well as being able to conduct scientific experiments, he is multi-lingual **(Chapters 6 and 12)**, a musician **(Chapter 8)**, a sportsman **(Chapter 5)**, a philosopher **(Chapters 2 and 7)** and a master of disguise – the seafarer **(Chapter 9)**.

- **Chapters 9 and 12:** We learn he does not trust women and he says he will never marry.

Five key quotations

1. Holmes: 'My mind rebels at stagnation.'
2. Watson on Holmes: 'our companion maintained his impenetrable reserve'
3. Holmes: 'My dear Watson, try a little analysis yourself ... You know my methods. Apply them'
4. Holmes on the Smiths: 'The main thing with people of that sort ... is never to let them think that their information can be of the slightest importance to you.'
5. Watson: 'He ... busied himself all the evening in an abstruse chemical analysis which involved much heating of retorts and distilling of vapors'

Note it!

As Dr Watson is the **first-person narrator** of the story, we see Sherlock Holmes from his point of view. Without direct access to Holmes's thoughts and feelings, the reader learns about his **character** through the information Watson provides about him. He therefore remains an enigma.

Exam focus

How can I write about Sherlock Holmes's character?

You can comment upon Holmes's relationship with other characters.

Holmes often sees it as his role to instruct others.	Clear focus on character
Conan Doyle shows that this is a particularly important part of his relationship with Dr Watson when, in Chapter 6, Holmes suggests Watson 'try a little analysis' himself.	Offers specific example
Holmes goes on to add rather bluntly 'you know my methods. Apply them.'	Provides further relevant support
The use of the imperatives 'try' and 'apply' in Holmes's speech also reveals his impatience and arrogance to the reader.	Analysis of language explains effect on reader

Now you try!

Finish this paragraph about Holmes's character. Use one of the quotations from the list.

Holmes's keen interest in the latest scientific methods is revealed by Conan Doyle when ....

My progress Needs more work ☐ Getting there ☐ Sorted! ☐

CHARACTERS Dr Watson

Five key things about Dr Watson

1. **Dr Watson** is the **narrator** of the story and the **reader's guide** to the events of the **novel**.
2. His exact **role** in Holmes's investigative work varies: sometimes he is an **assistant** and at others times he is a **fellow expert** or even a companion.
3. He can use his **specialist medical and military training** to help with cases.
4. Unlike Holmes, he **shows emotion** and can be **uncertain of himself**.
5. He is a **romantic character** whose behaviour towards **Miss Morstan** is **caring**, **compassionate** and **gentlemanly**.

What do we learn about Watson at the beginning of the novel?

- Watson lives with Holmes in Baker Street, London and assists him in his work.
- While he admires Holmes greatly, he is concerned about Holmes's drug use.
- He is a trained army doctor who was forced to retire after receiving a bullet wound to his leg during military service in Afghanistan.
- He has already published an account of one of Holmes's celebrated cases, *A Study in Scarlet*.
- He is sensitive and quick to defend his dead brother when Holmes deduces he was an alcoholic.

How does Dr Watson's character develop?

- **Chapter 2:** As Watson's feelings for Miss Morstan deepen, he becomes increasingly worried about his own low social status.
- **Chapters 3 and 7:** He is very protective of Mary and his first thoughts are always for her welfare.
- **Chapter 8:** He promises to recover the treasure even though it would effectively block his relationship with Mary.
- **Chapter 10:** He is more anxious than Holmes at times, e.g. feeling sick after the boat chase when he thinks of the **'horrible death'** they narrowly escaped. Despite his fears, however, he is determined to solve the mystery.
- **Chapter 10:** He is thrilled by the excitement of the river chase and, along with Holmes, fires his pistol at Tonga.

Five key quotations

1. Watson's medical view of Holmes's drug use: 'it is a pathological and morbid process which involves increased tissue-change and may ... leave a permanent weakness'
2. Watson's interest in the case: 'I don't think I could rest until I know more of this fantastic business.'
3. Watson on his low status: 'Might she not look upon me as a mere vulgar fortune-seeker?'
4. Watson's excitement: 'never did sport give me such a wild thrill as this mad, flying man-hunt down the Thames'
5. Watson on Mary: 'Whoever had lost a treasure, I knew that night that I had gained one.'

Note it!

Conan Doyle shows Watson's very romantic view of women. His descriptions of Miss Morstan's vulnerability at Pondicherry Lodge (Chapter 5) and her angelic beauty (Chapter 11) convey his growing regard for her, but also reveal wider Victorian attitudes to women as powerless to act.

Exam focus

How can I write about Dr Watson's character? AO1

You can use Watson's character to explore the theme of wealth.

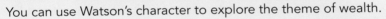

Watson seeks love, not wealth and this contrasts with other characters who are corrupted by money. This is shown by his comment in Chapter 11: 'Whoever had lost a treasure, I knew that night that I had gained one.' Here the contrast of the verbs 'lost' and 'gained' and the use of the treasure metaphor to refer to Mary emphasises that, for Watson, love has a far greater value than money.

- Clear focus on character
- Relevant support
- Detailed analysis of language
- Link to theme

Now you try!

Finish this paragraph about Dr Watson's character. Use one of the quotations from the list.

Watson's sense of care and responsibility for Holmes is revealed by Conan Doyle when ....

CHARACTERS Miss Morstan

Five key things about Miss Morstan

1. **Mary** is the person who brings the **'Sign of the Four' case** to Holmes and Watson.
2. She is clearly **attracted to Watson** from the start.
3. Her **financial circumstances** would **improve dramatically** if the **Agra treasure** is found.
4. She is **not motivated by money**, keeping the valuable pearls when she could have sold them.
5. Her **bravery and goodness** contrast with the behaviour of others in the **novel**.

What do we learn about Miss Morstan at the beginning of the novel?

- Mary is an orphan; her mother is dead and, as her father was an army captain in India, she grew up in a residential school in Edinburgh.
- The mysterious disappearance of her father ten years ago still causes her great pain.
- Mary has to earn her own living as a governess. She has lived a **'retired life'** and has **'no friends'** in London.
- She impresses both Watson *and* Holmes with her excellent organisation and clear understanding of the case.

How does Miss Morstan's character develop?

- **Chapter 3:** Mary copes bravely with the mysterious meeting followed by the night-time journey to the Sholto house and Pondicherry Lodge.
- **Chapter 4:** She grows in confidence and determination, interrupting Thaddeus Sholto and telling him to hurry up and make his story **'as short as possible'**.
- **Chapter 4:** She handles the news of her father's death with dignity, despite the cruel and sudden way Thaddeus tells her of it.
- **Chapter 5:** She considers the welfare of others before her own by looking after the terrified housekeeper following the discovery of the murder at Pondicherry Lodge.
- **Chapter 11:** Her feelings for Watson develop after the night of the murder, but she is careful not to reveal them until he confesses his love.

Five key quotations

1. Watson on Mary: 'She must have been more than woman if she did not feel some uneasiness ... yet her self-control was perfect'

2. Mary's confidence when addressing Thaddeus Sholto: 'It is very late, and I should desire the interview to be as short as possible.'

3. Watson on the Agra treasure: 'Miss Morstan ... would change from a needy governess to the richest heiress in England.'

4. Watson on his feelings for Mary: 'So we stood hand in hand, like two children, and there was peace in our hearts for all the dark things that surrounded us.'

5. Mary's reaction on opening the iron box: '"The treasure is lost," said Miss Morstan calmly.'

Note it!

Conan Doyle keeps Mary, the main female **character**, away from the dangerous action of the novel after the events at Pondicherry Lodge. At the end, when Holmes learns of Watson's proposed marriage, Mary is not there. This reflects Victorian ideas about women as passive.

Exam focus

How can I write about Mary's character? AO1

You can comment upon how Conan Doyle presents Mary through Watson.

> Conan Doyle presents the positive effect Mary has on Watson when, before the murder is discovered, they suddenly hold hands: like two children, and there was peace in our hearts for all the dark things that surrounded us'. Mary's innocent, calming nature is shown first by the simile and then the noun 'peace' which contrasts with the 'dark' events to come. Later, the housekeeper is also comforted by her.

Topic sentence with focus on character

Section of quotation fully integrated

Analysis of language and effects

Further example to develop point

Now you try!

Finish this paragraph about Mary's role in the novel. Use one of the quotations from the list.

At the end, Conan Doyle uses Mary's character to explore the theme of wealth through her reaction ....

My progress Needs more work ☐ Getting there ☐ Sorted! ☐   35

Five key things about Thaddeus Sholto

1. Thaddeus and his **twin brother, Bartholomew Sholto**, are **heirs to Major Sholto's fortune**.

2. He lives a **cultured, isolated life** surrounded by art and exotic objects, but he is **scared by real life** and, it seems, his brother.

3. It was **Thaddeus's idea** to **send the pearls to Mary** and to divide the treasure.

4. He is a **nervous hypochondriac** who sometimes behaves thoughtlessly, e.g. when he bluntly reveals to Mary that her father, Captain Morstan, is dead.

5. He **argued with his brother** about the **treasure** and was the last person to see him alive.

What is Thaddeus Sholto's function in the novel?

- Through Thaddeus we learn the story of Major Sholto's return from India with the treasure and, through his retelling of his father's dying statement, the details of Captain Morstan's death.

- His behaviour is contrasted with that of his brother and represents the **theme** of duality.

- At Pondicherry Lodge he becomes terrified that he **'shall be suspected'** of his brother's murder and his reactions contrast with the calm **character** of Miss Morstan.

- He is the first person arrested in the police investigation.

How does Thaddeus's character respond to events in the novel?

- **Chapter 4:** When the treasure is found, it is Thaddeus who insists Mary is a **'wronged woman'** and should have her share.

- **Chapter 4:** When he first meets Holmes and Watson he is agitated and mainly concerned about his own health.

- **Chapter 5:** He is terrified and helpless when Bartholomew's body is discovered.

- **Chapter 6:** When Jones arrests him he is desperate for Holmes and Watson to help him.

Five key quotations

1. Thaddeus on his home: 'An oasis of art in the howling desert of South London.'
2. Watson on Thaddeus: 'he was in an ecstasy of fear'
3. Thaddeus's argument with Bartholomew: 'It was all that I could do to ... send her a detached pearl at fixed intervals so at least [Miss Morstan] might never feel destitute.'
4. Watson on Thaddeus: 'He ... had the helpless appealing expression of a terrified child'
5. Thaddeus after the body is found: 'I know that I shall go mad!'

Note it!

In Chapter 11, Conan Doyle shows Mary Morstan's relief about the loss of the treasure, but the reader never sees Thaddeus Sholto's reaction to his lost fortune. His last appearance in the story is the mention of his release from custody in the newspaper report in Chapter 9.

Exam focus

How can I write about Thaddeus's character? AO1

You can comment upon how Thaddeus's actions provide a contrast to those of other characters.

After the murder Conan Doyle shows that Thaddeus is a weak character who needs protection. This is shown	Topic sentence about character
when Watson says he 'had the helpless, appealing expression of a terrified child'. The adjectives 'helpless'	Clear support
and 'terrified' and the metaphor about his child-like appearance provide a counterpoint to the calmness	Analysis of language and effects
of Mary's response. The characters of Thaddeus and Mary therefore do not fit masculine and feminine Victorian stereotypes.	Point about Victorian context

Now you try!

Finish this paragraph about Thaddeus's character. Use one of the quotations from the list.

Conan Doyle contrasts Thaddeus's caring nature with his twin brother's unfeeling nature when ....

CHARACTERS Jonathan Small

Five key things about Jonathan Small

1. Small is a **one-legged ex-soldier** who, along with the rest of **the Four**, steals the Agra treasure.

2. His sufferings as a **convict** and his experiences of **Major Sholto's betrayal** have left him with a **bitter sense of injustice**.

3. He is a **contradictory character** who can be **loyal and honest** yet also **cruel and violent**.

4. He is, however, very **protective of his devoted associate, Tonga**.

5. Overall his actions lead **directly** to the **deaths of two men** (the merchant **Achmet** and a **convict guard**) and **indirectly** to the **deaths of both Bartholomew and Major Sholto**.

What is Jonathan Small's significance in the novel?

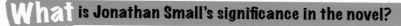

- **Chapter 10:** Jonathan Small, a **'wooden-legged man'**, makes his first appearance, but he does not speak directly until **Chapters 11 and 12**, thereby increasing **suspense**.

- **Chapters 11 and 12:** His account draws together many of the **novel's themes**: duality, crime and justice, wealth, and love and friendship.

- **Chapter 12:** He provides important details about the events which led to the theft of the treasure and the creation of the Sign of the Four.

- **Chapter 12:** By throwing the treasure into the River Thames he removes the barrier of wealth between Miss Morstan and Dr Watson.

How does Small's story alter our views of his character?

- The details of the crocodile attack, how Small was later forced to co-operate with the robbery and of his harsh life as a prisoner in a **'dreary, fever-stricken'** convict colony make the reader consider him more sympathetically.

- Small's fierce and absolute loyalty to his fellow criminals – Mahomet Singh, Dost Akbar and Abdullah Khan – is in stark contrast to Major Sholto's act of betrayal.

- His description of Tonga's faithfulness in Chapter 12 contradicts with the animalistic way Watson describes the Islander in Chapter 10.

Five key quotations

1. Watson on Small: 'more sorrow than anger in his rigid and contained countenance'
2. Small's loyalty: 'It's been the sign of four with us always.'
3. Small's sense of injustice: 'I would rather swing a score of times ... than feel that another man is at ease in a palace with the money that should be mine.'
4. Cruelty in Small: 'I thought of the treasure, and my heart set as hard as a flint'
5. Small on Major Sholto: 'A hundred times I have killed him in my sleep.'

Note it!

Small's wooden leg is a **symbol** of both crime and justice: it marks him out initially as a victim, but then it becomes a weapon to kill the convict guard. Finally, it is used to track Small down and, after the river chase, traps him in the mud.

Exam focus

How can I write about Jonathan Small's character? AO1

You can comment on how Small's character reflects the themes of the novel.

Jonathan Small is a character motivated by a burning sense of injustice. This is shown when he states	Topic sentence about character
he would rather 'swing a score of times' than have another living 'at ease in a palace' with his money. The	Relevant support
juxtaposing images of the condemned prisoner and the palace	Analysis of language
are shocking and make the reader question who, if anyone, in the novel has a right to the Agra treasure.	Effect on the reader

Now you try!

Finish this paragraph about Jonathan Small's character. Use one of the quotations from the list.

The contradictions in Small's character are shown when Watson comments

....

Five key things about Athelney Jones

1. Jones is a **respected Scotland Yard police detective**.
2. He has called upon **Sherlock Holmes's help** before.
3. He appears too **quick to make judgements** – and arrests.
4. He is shown to be very **concerned about his professional and public reputation**.
5. His concern with **facts** and his **over-bearing personality** make him a very different investigator to Holmes.

What is Jones's function in the novel?

- Jones reflects the **theme** of crime and justice by representing conventional police work. He acts as a **counterpoint** to Holmes's **character** with '**no room for theories**'; we learn more about how unusual Holmes's approach is when compared with that of the detective.
- Jones's offer of police officers and the steam-launch make the story of the river chase possible and even more dramatic.
- His involvement in events as a police detective makes the **novel** a **crime story** rather than just a mystery.
- Jones's arrest of Jonathan Small provides a **resolution** to the crime story.

How does Jones's character develop?

- **Chapter 6:** When he is first introduced Jones is over-confident and unwilling to listen to others' opinions or theories.
- **Chapter 8:** The first newspaper account of events, which Jones supplies to the paper, heaps praise on Jones's work and the '**prompt and energetic actions**' of the detective force.
- **Chapter 9:** When a second newspaper article reports that Thaddeus's arrest was a mistake, Jones becomes less sure of his methods.
- **Chapter 9:** After this, he is more humble and admits he needs Holmes's help.
- **Chapter 9:** Although Jones and Holmes argue about the best approach to the river chase, Jones does take Holmes's advice. Afterwards Jones is quick to take credit for Small's arrest (**Chapter 11**), but does at least thank Holmes in the end (**Chapter 12**).

Five key quotations

1. Jones's approach to his work: 'Let us apply common sense to the matter.'
2. Jones making a hasty decision: 'The card is some hocus-pocus,–a blind, as like as not.'
3. Watson's ironic comment on Jones: 'the brusque and masterful professor of common sense'
4. Jones's sense of fairness: 'If we are pretty quick in catching our men, we are not so quick in condemning them.'
5. Jones to Holmes: 'we all know that you are a connoisseur of crime, but duty is duty'

Note it!

Jones catches the spy in Pondicherry Lodge, Lal Rao, by accident. Conan Doyle uses a fishing **metaphor** in Chapter 12 when Holmes notes that at least Jones **'caught one fish'**, which perhaps mocks Jones's arrogant reference to his own **'net'** in Chapter 6.

Exam focus

How can I write about Jones's character? AO1

You can comment upon how Conan Doyle uses Jones to explore the theme of justice.

The character of Jones represents the public forces of law and order in the novel. Although Jones's character can appear arrogant, Conan Doyle ultimately shows that he is fair. After Small's capture Jones says that although the police might be 'quick' to catch men 'we are not so quick in condemning them' and his use of parallel phrasing here and the powerful verb 'condemn' reassures the reader that justice will be done.

Focus on character

Clear point

Integrated quotation

Analysis of technique

Now you try!

Finish this paragraph about the function of Jones's character. Use one of the quotations from the list.

Conan Doyle reveals the contrast between Jones and Holmes when Jones says to Holmes ....

Three key things about Bartholomew Sholto

1. Bartholomew is the **twin brother of Thaddeus Sholto** and the only other child of Major Sholto: the **'favourite one'**, according to Thaddeus.
2. He lives in his father's house, **Pondicherry Lodge**, and discovers the **Agra treasure** hidden there.
3. He is **murdered with a poisoned dart** and his body is discovered by Holmes and Watson in his room at Pondicherry Lodge.

What is his function in the novel?

- He acts as a direct contrast to his brother Thaddeus – the brothers and their very different natures reflect the **theme** of duality in the **novel**.
- His hoarding of the treasure reflects his **'father's fault'** of greed and represents the theme of wealth and its effects.
- The vivid description of his death creates a tense atmosphere of **Gothic** horror.

Three key things about Tonga

1. Tonga is a **native of the Andaman Islands** in the Bay of Bengal. These islands were used as a convict colony after the Indian Mutiny of 1857.
2. He is **saved from dying by Jonathan Small** who tends him during his illness; in return he **helps Small escape** from the islands and remains **'devoted' to him** afterwards.
3. He is responsible for the **murder of Bartholomew Sholto**.

What is his function in the novel?

- The circumstances in which Tonga breaks into Pondicherry Lodge and kills Bartholomew Sholto are the central mystery in the novel.
- He is described as a monstrous savage by both Watson and Holmes and this reflects Victorian attitudes to colonised peoples.
- His devotion to Small is an example of loyal friendship.

Five key quotations

1. Thaddeus on Bartholomew's greed: 'The pearls were evidently of great value, and he was averse to part with them'

2. Watson on the murder: 'The features were set ... in a horrible smile, a fixed and unnatural grin'

3. Holmes on Tonga: '[his] savage instincts ... had broken out'

4. Watson on Tonga: 'Never have I seen features so deeply marked with all bestiality and cruelty.'

5. Small on Tonga: 'He was stanch and true ... No man ever had a more faithful mate.'

Note it!

Bartholomew is murdered in his room which doubles up as a well-equipped laboratory (Chapter 5). His interest in chemical analysis mirrors Holmes's own experiments in Chapter 9 and reflects the popularity of amateur science in the Victorian period.

Exam focus

How can I write about context? (AO3)

You can use Tonga's character to discuss the context of the British Empire.

> Watson's descriptions of Tonga reveal Victorian attitudes to other races. Watson sees Tonga for the first time during the river chase and he immediately judges him as dangerous and uncivilised. This is shown when he describes Tonga's features as being 'marked with all bestiality and cruelty'. The linking of the two nouns, suggesting animalistic qualities, with the verb 'marked' reveals how Victorians often characterised non-white peoples as sub-human and morally stained.

Focus on character and context

Development of point

Support with integrated quotation

Analysis with language terms

Now you try!

Finish this paragraph about Bartholomew's character. Use one of the quotations from the list.

Conan Doyle explores the theme of wealth through Bartholomew Sholto's character when ....

1. Look at this ideas map representing the **character** of Sherlock Holmes. Is there anything else you could add?

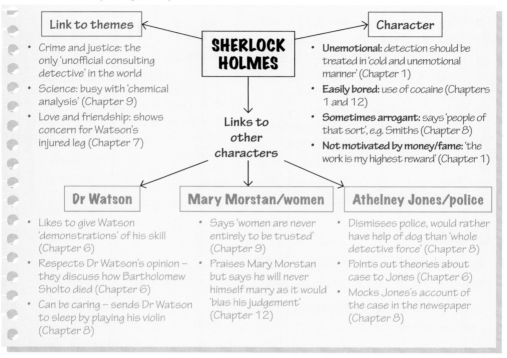

Link to themes

- Crime and justice: the only 'unofficial consulting detective' in the world
- Science: busy with 'chemical analysis' (Chapter 9)
- Love and friendship: shows concern for Watson's injured leg (Chapter 7)

SHERLOCK HOLMES

Character

- **Unemotional:** detection should be treated in 'cold and unemotional manner' (Chapter 1)
- **Easily bored:** use of cocaine (Chapters 1 and 12)
- **Sometimes arrogant:** says 'people of that sort', e.g. Smiths (Chapter 8)
- **Not motivated by money/fame:** 'the work is my highest reward' (Chapter 1)

Links to other characters

Dr Watson

- Likes to give Watson 'demonstrations' of his skill (Chapter 6)
- Respects Dr Watson's opinion – they discuss how Bartholomew Sholto died (Chapter 6)
- Can be caring – sends Dr Watson to sleep by playing his violin (Chapter 8)

Mary Morstan/women

- Says 'women are never entirely to be trusted' (Chapter 9)
- Praises Mary Morstan but says he will never himself marry as it would 'bias his judgement' (Chapter 12)

Athelney Jones/police

- Dismisses police, would rather have help of dog than 'whole detective force' (Chapter 8)
- Points out theories about case to Jones (Chapter 6)
- Mocks Jones's account of the case in the newspaper (Chapter 8)

2. Create your own ideas map for one of the other main characters.

Quick quiz

Answer these quick questions about the characters in the novel:

1. What was the name Watson gave to the previous case he and Holmes worked on together?
2. 'They are out of their depths': who says this about whom?
3. Who comes to visit Holmes and Watson at Baker Street to ask for help?
4. Who can be described as a romantic figure?
5. Who lives a cultured, isolated life on the edge of the city?
6. What shocking information does he thoughtlessly reveal to Mary?

7. What is the name of his twin brother?
8. Whose idea is it to send the pearls to Mary?
9. Whose body is discovered at Pondicherry Lodge? How did he die?
10. What is the name of the wooden-legged man identified by Holmes?
11. What does Watson think will block his relationship with Mary?
12. Where does the Islander come from?
13. Who does Athelney Jones arrest first for the murder of Bartholomew?
14. Who dresses up as a seafarer in Chapter 9?
15. Whose betrayal has left Small with 'a bitter sense of injustice'?
16. Who kills the convict guard and with what?
17. What treasure does Dr Watson say he has gained?
18. What name is missing from this list of the Sign of the Four: Jonathan Small, Abdullah Khan, Dost Akbar and …?
19. Who describes who as his 'faithful mate'?
20. Who says he 'will never marry'?

Power paragraphs

Write a paragraph in response to **each of these questions**. For each, try to **use one quotation** you have learned from this section.

1. How do the characters of the Sholto twins reflect the theme of duality?
2. Why does Conan Doyle choose to have Dr Watson wait until the treasure is lost before he proposes to Mary?

Exam practice

Re-read the section at the opening of Chapter 9 from 'It was late in the afternoon' to '"I shall be back in an hour or two," I remarked', where Watson and Holmes wait for further news and developments in the case.

What does this moment in the novel reveal about the differences between the two characters? Write **two paragraphs** explaining your ideas. You could comment upon:

- how both characters' appearance and actions are described
- how their different attitudes to women are shown.

Five key things about the theme of crime and justice

1. **Sherlock Holmes** is a **new type of detective** whose **scientific methods** of solving crimes are shown to be very different to those the police use.

2. Holmes is initially consulted by **Miss Morstan** about a **mysterious letter** which mentions **'justice'**; the investigation which follows leads to the discovery of actual crimes such as the **death of Bartholomew Sholto** and the **theft of the Agra treasure**.

3. The **police force** is represented by **Athelney Jones** and his men; Holmes, however, prefers initially to use his own alternative police force of street children – the **Baker Street Irregulars**.

4. **Jonathan Small** seeks **justice for himself and his three associates,** namely the return of the stolen Agra treasure.

5. **The Four** have already been **convicted** and harshly punished – by transportation to the **convict colony of the Andaman Islands** – for the initial crime of stealing the treasure.

Where are crime and punishment significant in the story?

- The theft of the treasure results in three murders (Achmet, the convict guard and Bartholomew Sholto) plus other related deaths (Major Sholto, Captain Morstan and then Tonga in the river chase). This makes the criminal investigation far more dramatic for the reader.

- The motivation for the criminal acts in the **novel** is a desire for wealth. The treasure is therefore seen to be a corrupting and criminal influence.

- The ineffectiveness of the police force acts as a **counterpoint** to Holmes's investigation, thus highlighting his special powers.

How are ideas of justice explored?

- The fate of Small and his punishment raises questions about justice.
- The death of Captain Morstan, although accidental, appears unjust.
- By the end of the novel the crimes are solved, but the treasure is lost forever, perhaps representing a form of justice.

Five key quotations

1. Thaddeus's letter to Mary: 'You are a wronged woman, and shall have justice'
2. Holmes: 'We shall work the case out independently, and leave this fellow Jones to exult over any mare's-nest which he may choose to construct.'
3. Holmes on the Sign of the Four: 'a sign that it was not a common murder, but ... something in the nature of an act of justice'
4. Holmes on the Baker Street Irregulars: 'They can go everywhere, see everything, overhear everyone.'
5. Small to Jones: 'Where is the justice that I should give [the treasure] up to those who have never earned it?'

Note it!

'Detectives' were first employed by the Metropolitan Police in the1840s. In the novel the police detectives are initially presented as foolish, and it is only when Holmes joins forces with them (Chapter 10) that the criminals are caught.

Exam focus

How can I write about the theme of crime and justice? AO1

You can explore the theme of crime using the police.

Conan Doyle presents the theme of crime through the police's misguided investigation. After the murder, Holmes says he will work 'independently' and leave Athelney Jones 'to exult over any mare's-nest which he may choose to construct'. The use of the verb 'exult' suggests Jones's arrogance and the slang 'mare's-nest', meaning muddle, emphasises to the reader that these crimes will only be solved by Holmes, a detective with new rigorous methods.

- Focus on the theme
- Specific support through quotation
- Analysis of language
- Development of point

Now you try!

Finish this paragraph about the theme of justice. Use one of the quotations from the list.

The Sign of the Four *itself symbolises the theme of justice, as is shown* ....

Five key things about the theme of love and friendship

1. Although they are very different **characters**, the **friendship between Holmes and Watson** is shown to be based upon **mutual respect** and a **shared sense of purpose**.

2. Unlike Watson, **Holmes** has **no interest** in the **emotional** or **romantic side of life**.

3. The **attraction between Miss Morstan and Dr Watson** is **immediate**.

4. **Loyalty** is shown to be very significant in the **novel**: **Jonathan Small** always remains **loyal** to the other **members of the Four**.

5. After his life has been saved by Small, **Tonga** is **devoted** to him; **Small**, in return, is **equally loyal** to his Islander friend.

How are friendship and loyalty explored in the story?

- **Chapters 1 and 6:** The relationship between Holmes and Watson can appear like that of a teacher and student when Holmes demonstrates and explains his methods.

- **Chapters 1, 7 and 8:** The novel opens with Watson's concern for Holmes's drug use. Later, Holmes is anxious about Watson's injured leg and his exhaustion. This shows the care which underlies their friendship.

- **Chapter 12:** After the theft of the treasure at Agra, Small remains committed to securing equal shares of the money for himself along with Mahomet Singh, Abdullah Khan and Dost Akbar.

- **Chapter 12:** Small is moved by Tonga's absolute devotion to him: **'[he] would do anything to serve me'**.

How does romance add to the plot?

- When (in Chapter 12) Watson announces his engagement to Mary he is disappointed by Holmes's response. Holmes insists he will never marry because emotion would interfere with his work.

- As the love between Watson and Mary deepens, the treasure is seen as a **'golden barrier'** between them. This **romance plot** contrasts with other relationships in the novel that are driven solely by the treasure, not by love.

Five key quotations

1. Watson on love: 'A wondrous subtle thing is love, for here were we two who had never seen each other before that day ... in an hour of trouble our hands instinctively sought for each other.'

2. Watson's view of Holmes: 'something of the air of a clinical professor expounding to his class'

3. Watson on Mary: 'Might she not look upon me as a mere vulgar fortune-seeker?'

4. Small on friendship: 'It's been the sign of the four with us always.'

5. Small about Tonga: 'He was stanch and true ... No man ever had a more faithful mate.'

Note it!

The most significant act of disloyalty in the novel involves Major Sholto. His betrayal of Small and the Four, and his refusal to share the treasure equally with them, leads to his argument with Captain Morstan and, indirectly, to Morstan's death.

Exam focus

How can I write about the theme of friendship? (AO1)

You can use the character of Small to explore the theme of friendship.

The character of Jonathan Small is used by Conan Doyle to present the theme of friendship and the importance of loyalty.	Focus on the theme
Small explains his motivation to Holmes and Watson in Chapter 12, saying: 'It's been the sign of the four with us always.'	Specific support through quotation
The use of the inclusive pronoun 'us' and the adverb 'always' emphasises the unbreakable bond between the Four who, despite being criminals, are	Analysis of language
utterly loyal to each other.	Development of point

Now you try!

Finish this paragraph about friendship. Use one of the quotations from the list.

The teacher–student relationship between Holmes and Watson is clearly shown by ....

Five key things about the theme of wealth

1. **Wealth** is **not presented positively** at any point the **novel**, but it does affect different **characters** in different ways.

2. **Money** appears to be **unimportant to Holmes and Watson**, although Watson does become more aware of his low income when he meets Mary who, if the treasure is found, would become a very rich woman.

3. Two characters are shown to be significantly **corrupted by wealth**: **Major Sholto** and his son **Bartholomew**.

4. **Jonathan Small** agrees to help **steal the treasure** after **Abdullah Khan** threatens him with death; later he wants to recover it to ensure that the Four receive their **fair share**.

5. The **Agra treasure** is eventually **lost forever** in the Thames, and so no one ever benefits from this stolen wealth.

Why is wealth significant in the story as a whole?

- The theft of the treasure and the distribution of this wealth is the main driver for the **crime story** of the novel.

- Wealth is seen as a **'golden barrier'** to love in the relationship between Watson and Mary; this reflects the rigid class structure in Victorian Britain.

- The Agra treasure connects the crime to events in the British Empire and Victorian attitudes to colonisation.

How do attitudes to wealth reveal characters' values?

- Major Sholto is shown to be greedy for wealth, and acts disloyally as a result of this.

- Bartholomew and Thaddeus Sholto argue about sending Miss Morstan the pearls. Bartholomew wants to keep them whereas Thaddeus is determined that Mary **'never feel destitute'**.

- Jonathan Small's attitude to wealth relates to the **theme** of justice: he does not want to see others profit from the treasure when the Four risked everything to obtain it.

- Mary is shown to value love over wealth when the loss of the treasure is discovered.

Five key quotations

1. Holmes: 'The work itself ... is my highest reward.'
2. Watson: 'What was I, an army surgeon with a weak leg and a weaker banking-account ... ?'
3. Major Sholto on Mary: 'The cursed greed which has been my besetting sin through life has withheld from her the treasure'
4. Captain Morstan's death: 'he fell backwards, cutting his head against the corner of the treasure-chest'
5. Small: 'I would rather swing a score of times ... than live in a convict's cell and feel that another man is at his ease in a palace with the money that should be mine.'

Note it!

The loss of the treasure (Chapter 10) solves the problem of who should keep this wealth. However, the treasure's Indian origins **symbolise** how the British Empire exploited the resources of its colonies and colonised peoples during the Victorian period.

Exam focus

How can I write about the theme of wealth? AO1

You can use the theme of wealth to explore plot structure.

The manner of Captain Morstan's death reflects the theme of wealth in the novel. As Morstan and Major Sholto argue over how the treasure should be divided, Morstan collapses, 'cutting his head against the treasure-chest'. Through this, Conan Doyle symbolises the corrupting power of wealth. This is also shown with the deaths of Achmet, Bartholomew Sholto and Tonga which all relate directly to the treasure.

- Focus on the theme
- Specific support through quotation
- Use of literary term
- Further development of point

Now you try!

Finish this paragraph about Major Sholto's greed. Use one of the quotations from the list.

Major Sholto shows how corrupted he has been by wealth when he admits that ....

THEMES Duality

Five key things about the theme of duality

1. The concept of **duality** – **opposing characteristics** which exist **alongside each other** – was an important one in **Victorian science and literature**.

2. Duality is a feature seen within the **character** of **Holmes**; his **'bad' drug use** is contrasted with his **'good' desire to solve crime**.

3. The **theme** is present in the character of **Jonathan Small** where his **criminal acts** are **contrasted** with his **care for Tonga**.

4. **Duality** is also seen in the personalities and behaviour of **pairs of characters** such as Holmes and Watson, the Sholto twins, Small and Tonga, and Major Sholto and Captain Morstan.

5. The contrast between **scientific logic** and **emotion**, which is a feature of the relationship between **Holmes** and **Watson**, is another example of duality.

How does duality relate to characters – Holmes and Watson?

- Conan Doyle's inclusion of Holmes's drug use at the beginning and end of the **novel** makes him appear a complex and enigmatic character.

- Watson's emotional response to Miss Morstan provides a contrast with Holmes's treatment of her as **'a mere unit,–a factor in a problem'** (Chapter 2).

- Holmes's considered and **'exact science'** of detection contrasts with Jones's rashness and traditional police detection methods.

Where is this theme significant for other characters?

- **Chapter 4:** Thaddeus's argument with his twin brother, Bartholomew, about the treasure and providing for Mary shows the stark difference between the two men.

- **Chapter 10:** The contrast between Watson's descriptions of the native Tonga and of Small reveals the Victorian view of native people as uncivilised and barbaric.

- **Chapter 12:** Small's nursing care for Tonga over **'a couple of months'**, which saved his life, **contrasts** with his brutal murder of the convict guard when he used his wooden leg as a weapon.

Five key quotations

1. Watson's concern for Holmes: 'Why should you, for a mere passing pleasure, risk the loss of those great powers with which you have been endowed?'

2. Holmes's criticism of Watson: 'The emotional qualities are antagonistic to clear reasoning.'

3. The discovery of Bartholomew's body: 'Looking straight at me ... there hung a face,–the very face of our companion Thaddeus.'

4. Small on caring for Tonga: 'He was sick to death ... I took him in hand ... and after a couple of months I got him right and able to walk.'

5. Watson's description of Tonga: 'this savage, distorted creature'

Note it!

Duality affects **settings** in the novel. The peaceful domestic interior of Mrs Forrester's **'tranquil English home'** contrasts with the earlier horrors of Pondicherry Lodge (Chapter 5) and with the later description of the **'wild and desolate'** river bank (Chapter 10).

Exam focus

How can I write about the theme of duality? (AO1)

You can use the theme of duality to explore characters.

Conan Doyle's characterisation of Sherlock Holmes reflects the theme of duality within a single character. Watson cannot understand how he can 'risk the loss of those great powers' for his drug use which he describes as a 'mere passing pleasure'. The contrast between the nouns 'powers' and 'pleasure' plus the plosive alliteration draw attention to the duality of Holmes's complex character in which both good and bad qualities co-exist.

- Focus on the theme
- Specific support through quotation
- Analysis of language
- Summarising comment

Now you try!

Finish this paragraph about duality and characters. Use one of the quotations from the list.

The duality of Holmes and Watson is shown by ....

My progress Needs more work ☐   Getting there ☐   Sorted! ☐   53

Five key things about the theme of science

1. The **novel** opens with **Holmes** providing a detailed explanation of the **'science of deduction'** to Watson.

2. **Dr Watson** and **Sherlock Holmes** have both had **extensive scientific training** – one as a medical doctor and the other as a self-taught 'scientific detective'.

3. Through his **precise scientific observation** of the murder scene at **Pondicherry Lodge**, **Holmes** begins to form a picture of **'the wooden-legged man'**, Jonathan Small, and his strange accomplice, Tonga.

4. Both **Holmes** and the deceased **Bartholomew Sholto** have **chemical laboratory apparatus** in their homes.

5. **Small** uses his understanding of **medical science** – gained from working with a surgeon in the Andaman Islands – to **cure Tonga**, and this act, indirectly, leads to his escape.

How does science relate to the structure of the story?

- The **theme** of science establishes Holmes as a detective with **'peculiar powers'**. With this, Conan Doyle creates a new type of **crime story** based on scientific principles of **'observation'** and **'deduction'**.

- Scientific analysis of evidence is important throughout the story, e.g. in Chapter 6 after the murder at Pondicherry Lodge.

- Holmes's treatment of all crime as a scientific problem leads the reader to expect a logical solution to every case.

How does this theme add to character development?

- Holmes's logical and unemotional **character** reflects his cold and rational approach to all human relationships, contrasting with Dr Watson's more emotional responses to events and people.

- Holmes's and Watson's shared discussions about science connect them as characters and form the basis of their friendship; their talk reflects a growing Victorian interest in scientific study.

- Holmes's precise scientific observations provide a **counterpoint** to the rash and foolish guesswork of Athelney Jones and the police, who are quick to make arrests and claim credit for solving the case.

Five key quotations

1. Watson on Holmes's methods: '[with] his lens and a tape measure … hurried about the room on his knees, measuring, comparing, examining'

2. Watson on Holmes's character: 'You really are an automaton,–a calculating-machine!'

3. Bartholomew's home laboratory: 'littered over with Bunsen burners, test-tubes, and retorts'

4. Watson on Holmes: 'busied himself all evening in an abstruse chemical analysis which involved much heating of retorts and distilling of vapors'

5. Holmes: 'Individuals vary, but percentages remain constant. So says the statistician.'

Note it!

There were incredible innovations and discoveries in science in the Victorian era. Great advances were made in medicine, chemistry, engineering, communications and travel. For example, the steam-powered boat in Chapter 10 reflects a scientific invention of the time.

Exam focus

How can I write about the theme of science? AO1

You can use the theme of science to explore characters.

Conan Doyle uses the theme of science to present Holmes's unusual methods and logical character. For example, Watson describes Holmes examining the crime scene at Pondicherry Lodge using a 'lens and tape measure' where he is 'measuring, comparing, examining' the room. The scientific instruments such as the magnifying lens plus the list of three verbs describing his observations reveal his precise methods of deduction which contrast with the more haphazard methods of the police.

- Topic sentence on the theme
- Specific support using quotation
- Analysis of language
- Conclusion about character

Now you try!

Finish this paragraph about context. Use one of the quotations from the list.

The description of Bartholomew Sholto's home laboratory as ....

1. Look at this ideas map representing the **theme** of love and friendship. Is there anything else you could add?

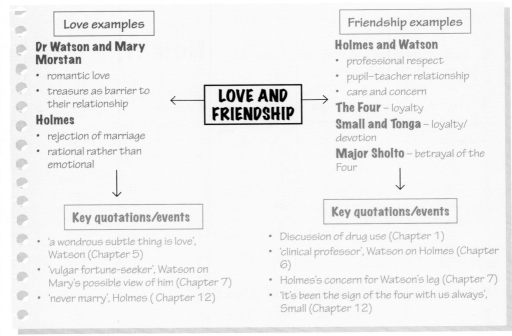

Love examples

Dr Watson and Mary Morstan
- romantic love
- treasure as barrier to their relationship

Holmes
- rejection of marriage
- rational rather than emotional

LOVE AND FRIENDSHIP

Friendship examples

Holmes and Watson
- professional respect
- pupil–teacher relationship
- care and concern

The Four – loyalty

Small and Tonga – loyalty/devotion

Major Sholto – betrayal of the Four

Key quotations/events
- 'a wondrous subtle thing is love', Watson (Chapter 5)
- 'vulgar fortune-seeker', Watson on Mary's possible view of him (Chapter 7)
- 'never marry', Holmes (Chapter 12)

Key quotations/events
- Discussion of drug use (Chapter 1)
- 'clinical professor', Watson on Holmes (Chapter 6)
- Holmes's concern for Watson's leg (Chapter 7)
- 'It's been the sign of the four with us always', Small (Chapter 12)

2. Create your own ideas map for one of the other themes.

Quick quiz

Answer these quick questions about the themes of the novel:

1. What is the 'golden barrier' between Watson and Mary?
2. The relationship between Holmes and Watson can sometimes appear like that between a teacher and …?
3. Which two characters in the novel are amateur scientists?
4. Why is Tonga so devoted to Jonathan Small?
5. What do the Sholto twins argue about before the murder of Bartholomew?
6. Where are Small and his three associates sent as punishment for the theft of the treasure?

7. What is the name Holmes gives to the alternative force of street children who help his investigation?
8. Who says: 'Whoever had lost a treasure, I knew that night I had gained one'?
9. Who is being described here: 'No man ever had a more faithful mate'?
10. Which of the Sholto twins shares his father's fault of greed?
11. What is meant by the word duality?
12. Who is described by Watson as full of 'fury and passion'?
13. What happens to the Agra treasure at the end of the novel?
14. Who retreats to his 'chemical analysis' when the investigation slows down?
15. What objects are sent to Mary from the Agra treasure?
16. Who murders Bartholomew Sholto?
17. Who is described as 'a calculating machine'?
18. How does Captain Morstan die?
19. How does Jonathan Small murder the convict guard?
20. Who says 'A wondrous subtle thing is love'?

Power paragraphs

Write a paragraph in response to **each of these questions**. For each, try to **use one quotation** you have learned from this section.

1. How does the character of Jonathan Small reflect the theme of wealth?
2. How does Conan Doyle use language to show Holmes's scientific skills and knowledge?

Exam practice

Re-read the section in Chapter 12 from 'I could not trust myself' to 'whether it is in my favor or not', where Jonathan Small describes the murder of the merchant Achmet.

How does Conan Doyle use language to present the violence of this crime? Write **two paragraphs** explaining your ideas. You could comment on:

- the way in which the merchant Achmet is described
- how Small's actions are presented.

LANGUAGE Imagery and vocabulary

Five key things about imagery and vocabulary

1. Conan Doyle uses **atmospheric Gothic descriptions** of **settings** both in **London** and in **India** to create an eerie, mysterious **tone**.

2. **Dialogue** is used in the **novel** to **reveal character**, e.g. Holmes's speech is factual and rational with complex **vocabulary**, whereas Mr Sherman uses cockney **dialect** which reflects his lower class.

3. **Precise scientific language** is used by both Holmes and Watson as they investigate the case.

4. **The Sign of the Four** is used as a recurrent **symbol** or **motif**.

5. **Sherlock Holmes** frequently **quotes from other writers** and uses **other languages**, showing his wide reading and **powerful intellect**.

Where is imagery in description significant in the story?

- **Chapters 3 and 5:** The detailed description of the image of the Sign of Four and its reappearance as a clue in the murder scene emphasises its importance to the story.

- **Chapters 4 and 5:** The night-time journey to Thaddeus's home and to Pondicherry Lodge uses **pathetic fallacy** where the gloomy settings and the **'wild dark business'** of the case create a sense of **foreboding**.

- **Chapter 12:** Jonathan Small's description of the old quarter of Agra **'where nobody goes'** and which is **'given over to the scorpions and centipedes'** creates a sense of menace and Gothic mystery.

How is vocabulary used for effect in dialogue?

- The discussion between Holmes and Watson about the exact cause of Bartholomew Sholto's death (Chapter 6) uses many precise medical terms reflecting both characters' scientific background.

- The difference between Holmes's speech and the cockney dialect of Mr Sherman (Chapter 7) shows the class difference between the two men.

- Holmes's reference to the German philosopher Richter on **'man's real greatness ... lies in his perception of his own smallness'** (Chapter 7) shows his deep understanding of a wide range of subjects and sets him apart from characters such as Athelney Jones.

Five key quotations

1. Watson on Thaddeus's house: 'lines of new staring brick buildings,— the monster tentacles which the giant city was throwing out into the country'

2. Mr Sherman threatens Holmes: 'I have a wiper in the bag, an' I'll drop it on your 'ead if you don't hook it.'

3. Watson's medical knowledge: 'Death from some powerful vegetable alkaloid ... some strychnine-like substance which would produce tetanus.'

4. Holmes on the Sign of the Four: 'four crosses in a line with their arms touching'

5. Small on the old quarter of Agra: 'full of great deserted halls, and winding passages, and long corridors'

Note it!

Small's wooden leg can be seen as a symbol. At first it presents him as a victim of the crocodile attack, but later Small admits he used his leg as a weapon to kill the convict guard. This implies Small's criminal acts are not entirely his fault.

Exam focus

How can I write about imagery and vocabulary? AO2

You can explore how symbols are used.

Conan Doyle's repeated use of the symbol of the 'Sign of the Four' is connected with the theme of friendship.	A focus on imagery
In Chapter 3 the sign is described as four crosses in a line with their arms touching'.	Relevant supporting quotation
The image, with its use of the personified 'arms touching', suggests the powerful connection between the men	Analysis of language
and it becomes a motif which reflects the unbreakable bond of loyalty between the Four.	Literary term leading to conclusion

Now you try!

Finish this paragraph about the use of dialogue to reveal character. Use one of the quotations from the list.

Mr Sherman is effectively characterised, through Conan Doyle's use of dialogue, when he threatens Holmes, saying ....

Five key things about narrative style and techniques

1. **Dr Watson** is a **first-person**, **frame narrator**; the reader is presented with all events through his eyes.

2. There are many **other texts** within the story: they include **letters**, **newspaper reports** and **testimonies** from other **characters**.

3. The **chronology** of the events in the **novel** is **just four days**, but there are **flashbacks** to much earlier events such as the siege at Agra.

4. The novel is a **crime story**, but it includes **Gothic** elements and even a **romance subplot**.

5. The novel **begins and ends with** the two main characters, **Holmes and Watson**.

What is significant about the narrative techniques?

- Dr Watson as the narrator is the reader's trustworthy guide and we follow him as his and our understanding of the case develops.

- Sometimes the events of the story happen quickly – the river chase (Chapter 10) occurs over just a few hours and is therefore dramatic. The events recounted by Small (Chapter 12) take place over years and provide a detailed background to the story.

- Using the two main characters, and Holmes's drug use, to both open and close the story creates a circular structure and emphasises their partnership.

Where are documents and aspects of genre important to the plot?

- The use of texts such as letters and newspaper reports provides different perspectives on and evidence for the criminal investigation.

- The crime story leads readers to expect investigators and criminals, the Gothic descriptions of **setting** increase the mystery and **suspense** and the romantic subplot provides a positive **counterpoint** to the dark events of the rest of the novel.

60

Five key quotations

1. Watson the narrator and author: 'a small brochure with the somewhat fantastic title of "A Study in Scarlet"'
2. Thaddeus's letter: 'You are a wronged woman, and shall have justice.'
3. Watson on the river chase: 'never did sport give me such a wild thrill as this mad, flying man-hunt down the Thames'
4. Watson using the language of romance: 'Whoever had lost a treasure, I knew that night that I had gained one.'
5. Small's flashback to the Indian Mutiny: 'From every point on the compass there was nothing but torture and murder and outrage.'

Quick quiz

Answer these quick questions about the language used in the novel.

1. Is the following an example of a simile or metaphor – 'the monster tentacles which the giant city was throwing out into the country'?
2. What is the term for an important symbol which is repeated in a story?
3. How does Conan Doyle's use of language present Sherlock Holmes as a well-educated and well-read character?
4. The murder of Bartholomew Sholto and the river chase both happen at night. What mood does this create for the reader?
5. What does Mr Sherman's use of dialect tell us about his character?
6. Apart from the crime story and Gothic elements, what other style of narrative does Conan Doyle use?
7. What type of narrator is Dr Watson?
8. Name two types of text, apart from Dr Watson's narrative, which tell the story.
9. What is the word used to describe the time over which a story takes place?
10. What is the term for a part of a story referring to earlier events?

Power paragraphs

Write a paragraph in response to **each of these questions**. For each, try to **use one quotation** you have learned from this section.

1. How does Conan Doyle use imagery to create a Gothic, eerie mood?
2. What specific language makes the river chase a dramatic climax?

Five key things about the exam

1. You will have **one** question on *The Sign of the Four* which will be based on a **passage** given to you on the exam paper.
2. It will focus on **Conan Doyle's presentation** of an aspect of the novel, such as a **character**, **relationship** or a **theme**.
3. You will have **45–50 minutes** to read and respond to the question.
4. The question is worth **30 marks**.
5. The question assesses **AOs 1, 2 and 3**. Remember that **AO3** relates to **'context'**.

What will a question look like?

1. Starting with this extract, explore how Conan Doyle presents Holmes as cold and unemotional.
   Write about:
   - how Conan Doyle presents Holmes as cold and unemotional in this extract
   - how Conan Doyle presents Holmes as cold and unemotional in the novel as a whole.
     [30 marks]

You must refer to the given passage

You must explain the techniques Conan Doyle uses

This is the area you must tackle

A reminder to begin with the given extract

A reminder to **also** write about the whole of the novel

Do all questions look the same?

- Not all questions will begin this way. Some might contain **statements** you must argue for or against, e.g. **'Conan Doyle presents Holmes as a very intelligent and arrogant character.' Starting with this extract, explore how far you agree with this opinion.**

- Not all questions will be about a **single character**. Some might ask you about a **relationship between two characters**, e.g. between Dr Watson and Miss Morstan.

What do I need to do to get a good mark?

Use this grid to understand your current level and how to improve it:

AO1 Read, understand, respond	AO2 Analyse language, form, structure and effects	AO3 Show understanding of contexts
High • You make **precise references** to the passage and *The Sign of the Four* **as a whole**. • Your argument is **well-structured**, with quotations **fluently embedded** in sentences. • You cover **both** the extract and the whole novel.	• You **analyse** and **interpret** the methods Conan Doyle uses **very effectively**. • You **explore thoughtfully** the effects of these on the reader. • You show **excellent use** of subject terminology.	• You make **detailed, relevant links** between specific elements of the novel and social and/ or historical contexts.
Mid • You make a **range of references** to the passage and the novel as a whole. • You respond in **a clear, logical way** with **relevant** quotations chosen.	• You **explain clearly** some of the methods Conan Doyle uses, and **some effects** on the reader. • You use **mostly relevant** subject terminology.	• You show **clear evidence** of understanding context which is **linked** to the novel in places.
Lower • You make **some references** to the passage and novel as a whole, but in rather a **patchy** way. • You make **some useful points** but evidence is **not always clear or relevant**.	• You make **occasional attempts** to explain Conan Doyle's methods but these are a little **unclear**. • You show **some use** of subject terminology.	• You demonstrate **basic awareness** of context but **links** to the novel are **undeveloped** and **not always relevant**.

Read this exam-style character question

Read this extract from Chapter 5 in which Holmes and Watson are discussing the discovery of Bartholomew Sholto's body. Then answer the question that follows.

> 'In God's name, what does it all mean?' I asked.
>
> 'It means murder,' said he, stooping over the dead man. 'Ah, I expected it. Look here!' He pointed to what looked like a long, dark thorn stuck in the skin just above the ear.
>
> 'It looks like a thorn,' said I.
>
> 5   'It is a thorn. You may pick it out. But be careful, for it is poisoned.'
>
> I took it up between my finger and thumb. It came away from the skin so readily that hardly any mark was left behind. One tiny speck of blood showed where the puncture had been.
>
> 'This is all an insoluble mystery to me,' said I. 'It grows darker instead of clearer.'
>
> 10   'On the contrary,' he answered, 'it clears every instant. I only require a few missing links to have an entirely connected case.'
>
> We had almost forgotten our companion's presence since we entered the chamber. He was still standing in the doorway, the very picture of terror, wringing his hands and moaning to himself. Suddenly, however, he broke out into a sharp, querulous cry.
>
> 15   'The treasure is gone!' he said. 'They have robbed him of the treasure! There is the hole through which we lowered it. I helped him to do it! I was the last person who saw him! I left him here last night, and I heard him lock the door as I came down-stairs.'
>
> 'What time was that?'
>
> 'It was ten o'clock. And now he is dead, and the police will be called in, and I shall be
>
> 20   suspected of having had a hand in it. Oh, yes, I am sure I shall. But you don't think so, gentlemen? Surely you don't think that it was I? Is it likely that I would have brought you here if it were I? Oh, dear! oh, dear! I know that I shall go mad!' He jerked his arms and stamped his feet in a kind of convulsive frenzy.
>
> 'You have no reason for fear, Mr. Sholto,' said Holmes, kindly, putting his hand upon
>
> 25   his shoulder. 'Take my advice, and drive down to the station to report this matter to the police. Offer to assist them in every way. We shall wait here until your return.'
>
> The little man obeyed in a half-stupefied fashion, and we heard him stumbling down the stairs in the dark.

2. Starting with this extract, explore how Conan Doyle presents Thaddeus Sholto's strange and unusual behaviour. Write about:

- how Conan Doyle presents Thaddeus's strange and unusual behaviour in this extract
- how Conan Doyle presents Thaddeus's strange and unusual behaviour in the novel as a whole. **[30 marks]**

NOW read this further character question

Read this extract from Chapter 12 in which Jonathan Small tells the story of his dealings with Major Sholto and his first meeting with Tonga. Then answer the question that follows.

> 'Well, gentlemen, I weary you with my long story, and I know that my friend Mr. Jones is impatient to get me safely stowed in chokey. I'll make it as short as I can. The villain Sholto went off to India, but he never came back again. Captain Morstan showed me his name among a list of passengers in one of the
> 5   mail-boats very shortly afterwards. His uncle had died, leaving him a fortune, and he had left the army, yet he could stoop to treat five men as he had treated us. Morstan went over to Agra shortly afterwards, and found, as we expected, that the treasure was indeed gone. The scoundrel had stolen it all, without carrying out one of the conditions on which we had sold him the secret. From
> 10   that day I lived only for vengeance. I thought of it by day and I nursed it by night. It became an overpowering, absorbing passion with me. I cared nothing for the law,–nothing for the gallows. To escape, to track down Sholto, to have my hand upon his throat,–that was my one thought. Even the Agra treasure had come to be a smaller thing in my mind than the slaying of Sholto.
> 15   'Well, I have set my mind on many things in this life, and never one which I did not carry out. But it was weary years before my time came. I have told you that I had picked up something of medicine. One day when Dr. Somerton was down with a fever a little Andaman Islander was picked up by a convict-gang in the woods. He was sick to death, and had gone to a lonely place to
> 20   die. I took him in hand, though he was as venomous as a young snake, and after a couple of months I got him all right and able to walk. He took a kind of fancy to me then, and would hardly go back to his woods, but was always hanging about my hut. I learned a little of his lingo from him, and this made him all the fonder of me.'

3. 'Conan Doyle presents Jonathan Small to the reader as both a good *and* a bad man.' Starting with this extract, explore how far you agree with this opinion. Write about:

   - how Conan Doyle presents Jonathan Small as both a good *and* a bad man in this extract

   - how Conan Doyle presents Jonathan Small as both a good *and* a bad man in the novel as a whole.

   [30 marks]

EXAM PRACTICE Planning your character response

Five key stages to follow

1. **Read** the **question**; **highlight** key words.
2. **Read** the **passage** with the **key words** from the **question** in mind.
3. Quickly **generate ideas** for your response.
4. **Plan** for paragraphs.
5. **Write** your response; **check it** against your plan as you progress.

What do I focus on?

Highlight the **key words**:

> 2. Starting with this extract, explore how Conan Doyle presents Thaddeus Sholto's strange and unusual behaviour. Write about:
> - how Conan Doyle presents Thaddeus's strange and unusual behaviour in this extract
> - how Conan Doyle presents Thaddeus's strange and unusual behaviour in the novel as a whole. **[30 marks]**

What do they tell you? Focus on Thaddeus Sholto's behaviour as the main topic; explain Conan Doyle's methods; focus on the extract and the whole text.

How should I read the passage?

- Check for any immediate links to the question (e.g. Thaddeus's silence while Holmes and Watson discuss the murder; his behaviour; what Thaddeus says).
- Look for any evidence or quotations you could highlight (e.g. **'wringing his hands and moaning to himself'**).

How do I get my ideas?

Note your ideas in a spider diagram or list them in a table:

The extract

Silence at beginning – shock, 'wringing his hands and moaning'

Focus on treasure, not his brother, 'the treasure is gone'

Concern mainly for himself, 'I know that I shall go mad'

Thaddeus's behaviour

The novel as a whole

Arranges strange meeting at Lyceum

Thoughtlessly tells Mary her father is dead

'hypochondriac' – according to Dr Watson

Wants Mary to have fair share of treasure, 'wronged woman', frightened of his twin

The extract	The novel as a whole
• Silence at beginning – also 'wringing his hands and moaning'	• Arranges meeting at Lyceum
	• Tells Mary her father is dead
• Focuses on treasure, not his brother, 'the treasure is gone'	• Is a 'hypochondriac' – according to Dr Watson
• Is concerned mainly for himself, 'I know that I shall go mad'	• Wants Mary to have fair share of treasure: 'wronged woman'

HOW do I structure my ideas?

Make a **plan** for **paragraphs**.*

- Paragraph 1: Go straight into your first point: *Thaddeus's silence and actions 'wringing his hands and moaning' are strange.*
- Paragraph 2: *Thaddeus's main concern is for himself as a possible suspect.*
- Paragraph 3: *Thaddeus's behaviour contrasts with that of others, e.g. Mary.*
- Paragraph 4: *He thoughtlessly tells Mary about her father's death in contrast with Watson's care for Mary.*
- Paragraph 5: *Thaddeus wants to share treasure with Mary, a 'wronged woman', unlike brother or father – links to who really deserves treasure?*

HOW do I write effectively?

Write **clear**, **analytical** paragraphs and **embed** evidence fluently, e.g.

Thaddeus is one of several characters who are selfish. He also acts as a counterpoint to other characters who instead show loyalty, love or friendship. In this extract, his unusual question to Holmes and Watson, 'Surely you don't think that it was I?', in relation to the murder, and Conan Doyle's use of a question and the adverb 'surely', reflect Thaddeus's anxiety and his very self-centred nature.	Overview links to extract
	Key term and link to rest of text
	Quotation embedded in sentence
	Analysis of language
	Summary point

Now you try!

Re-read Question 3 on page 65 and plan your response in the same way.

* The plan above and the sample answers on pages 68 and 70 have five paragraphs, but you don't need to be limited to this if you have more points to include (and time to write them!).

What does a Grade 5 answer look like?

Read the task again, then the sample answer below.

2. Starting with this extract, explore how Conan Doyle presents Thaddeus Sholto's strange and unusual behaviour. Write about:
   - how Conan Doyle presents Thaddeus's strange and unusual behaviour in this extract
   - how Conan Doyle presents Thaddeus's strange and unusual behaviour in the novel as a whole. **[30 marks]**

In the passage Thaddeus behaves in an unusual and strange way as he doesn't react to the murder of his brother. He does not speak and this is a contrast to Holmes and Watson who talk about the murder in detail and have 'almost forgotten' Thaddeus is there. Thaddeus is then described as a 'very picture of terror' and this phrase shows that he could be in shock about the death of his brother. The verbs 'wringing' and 'moaning' also show the serious effect the discovery has had upon him.

This behaviour might not seem very strange, but it is unusual when he speaks and he does not mention his brother and instead says 'the treasure is gone'. Conan Doyle therefore shows here that Thaddeus does not have a close relationship with his brother and they are almost opposites. This could relate to the Victorian interest in duality. Strange behaviour is also seen when Thaddeus is more concerned about what will happen to him. He repeats the word 'I' as he is more worried about how the crime will affect him and is terrified that he was 'the last person' to see Bartholomew alive. The reader then sees he could be a suspect in the murder investigation.

Conan Doyle also shows Thaddeus's strange reaction with 'O dear! O dear!' This is also shown by the verbs used to describe his movements: 'jerked' and 'stamped.' Thaddeus is therefore seen as a very emotional character in a 'convulsive frenzy'. He contrasts to other characters in this chapter, for example, Mary Morstan, who is very calm and concerned about the welfare of others and Holmes who remains controlled and unemotional.

AO1 Clear statement and link to question

AO2 Close reference to word use and what it means

AO1 Clear progression to next point

AO3 Link made to Victorian context, but not developed

AO2 Lack of analysis

AO2 Relevant idea but not developed sufficiently

AO2 Clear link made with evidence to structure used by Conan Doyle

Earlier in the novel, when Thaddeus meets Mary, his behaviour is unusual in that he tells her suddenly about her father's death without thinking about how this shocking news will affect her. He also is more concerned with his own health and asks Dr Watson about his symptoms – the doctor then calls him a 'hypochondriac'. This shows that Dr Watson is very critical of Thaddeus and worried about Mary. Dr Watson's very negative reaction to Thaddeus's behaviour is I think used by Conan Doyle to emphasise Watson's growing feelings for Mary.

Paragraph 4

Thaddeus's attitude to the treasure in the rest of the novel is also shown to be unusual compared to other characters. Thaddeus's father, Major Sholto, and his brother Bartholomew were more concerned with keeping the Agra treasure for themselves, but Thaddeus is determined that Mary should have her share and describes her as a 'wronged woman'. The word 'wronged' shows that Thaddeus knows that they have been unfair to her and I think Conan Doyle is saying to the reader that it isn't clear who really deserves the Agra treasure as it was stolen during the Indian Mutiny.

Paragraph 5

Check the skills

Re-read paragraphs four and five of this response and:

- highlight other **points** made
- circle any reference to **context**
- underline any places where the student has made an **interpretation**.

Now you try!

Look again at paragraph three ('*Conan Doyle also shows ...*') and improve it by:

- **Identifying** and **analysing** the unusual punctuation in **'O dear! O dear!'**
- **Explaining** what this tells us about Thaddeus's state of mind
- **Explaining** the significance of the phrase **'convulsive frenzy'**
- Ending with a **summary point** about how this shows Thaddeus's strange behaviour
- Improving the overall **style** by making sure your sentences **flow**; using **connectives** to **link** ideas

What does a Grade 7+ answer look like?

Read the task again, then the sample answer below.

2. Starting with this extract, explore how Conan Doyle presents Thaddeus Sholto's strange and unusual behaviour. Write about:
- how Conan Doyle presents Thaddeus's strange and unusual behaviour in this extract
- how Conan Doyle presents Thaddeus's strange and unusual behaviour in the novel as a whole.   **[30 marks]**

Conan Doyle's presentation of Thaddeus's strange and unusual behaviour is important, both in the extract and the novel as a whole, as it lightens the tone in some dark parts of the story and also contrasts with the actions of other characters. Initially in the extract Thaddeus's lack of action is strange, shown by his silence during Holmes's and Watson's detailed discussion of the murder. Thaddeus does not react to Holmes's references to the 'poisoned' thorn or 'speck of blood' and the verbs used by Conan Doyle to describe his behaviour – 'wringing his hands' and 'moaning' – make him seem ridiculous and also suggest that his 'terror' is for himself.

> **AO1** Clear statement sets out argument

> **AO2** Carefully selected evidence and detailed analysis of language use and effect

When Thaddeus actually does speak it is because of the loss of the treasure: 'They have robbed him ...!' The use of an exclamation mark here shows Thaddeus's surprise yet the verb 'robbed' is ironic because, as Conan Doyle shows elsewhere, the Agra treasure was stolen during the Indian Mutiny and Major Sholto's entire wealth, it seems, was similarly taken from British India.

> **AO1** Effective use of embedded quotation

> **AO2** Excellent language analysis

> **AO3** Appropriate use of context

Unusually, Thaddeus's main concern is how events will affect him as 'the last person' to see Bartholomew alive. The reader knows, according to the conventions of detective stories, he will become the first suspect in the criminal case. Thaddeus questions Holmes and Watson in an increasingly desperate way: 'Surely you don't think that it was I?' His fear of capture is self-centred but also accurate because, later in the novel, Conan Doyle uses Thaddeus's hasty arrest to demonstrate the foolishness of the police investigation.

> **AO3** Skilful link to genre context

> **AO3** Skilful link to another episode

Thaddeus's strange behaviour is reflected in his mental and physical weakness. This is shown by his 'convulsive frenzy' which suggests uncontrolled movements almost like a medical condition. This mirrors Thaddeus's introduction in the story as a 'confirmed hypochondriac' whose main care is his own welfare. In this way, Thaddeus's behaviour, before and after the murder, is used by Conan Doyle as a counterpoint to the controlled and calm behaviour of Mary which almost reverses the Victorian stereotype of the logical male and emotional female.

Paragraph 4

Finally, Thaddeus's generous behaviour in the novel is unusual when considered alongside the 'cursed greed' of his father and brother. Unlike them, he believed Mary was a 'wronged woman' and the use of the adjective 'wronged' shows Thaddeus's sense of justice and determination to secure Mary's rights. Conan Doyle thereby contrasts the character of Thaddeus with that of his twin. This use of opposite character types reflects a Victorian scientific interest in duality such as good and evil which, according to Holmes, makes man ultimately 'a strange enigma'.

Paragraph 5

Check the skills

Re-read paragraphs four and five of this response and:

- identify any particularly **fluent** or **well-expressed** ideas
- find any further references to **context**
- highlight any places where the student has shown **deeper insight** and offered **original** or particularly **thoughtful** ideas or made interesting **links**.

Now you try!

Now, using the plan you made for Question 3 on page 67, write a full response. Here's a reminder of the question:

3. 'Conan Doyle presents Jonathan Small to the reader as both a good *and* a bad man.' Starting with this extract, explore how far you agree with this opinion. Write about:
   - how Conan Doyle presents Jonathan Small as both a good *and* a bad man in this extract
   - how Conan Doyle presents Jonathan Small as both a good *and* a bad man in the novel as a whole. **[30 marks]**

Try to match your answer to the High Level objectives on page 63.

Read this exam-style theme question

Read this extract from Chapter 4 in which Thaddeus Sholto is explaining to Holmes and Watson how his brother found the hidden treasure at Pondicherry Lodge. Then answer the question that follows.

> Thaddeus Sholto talked incessantly, in a voice which rose high above the rattle of the wheels.
>
> 'Bartholomew is a clever fellow,' said he. 'How do you think he found out where the treasure was? He had come to the conclusion that it was somewhere
> 5 indoors: so he worked out all the cubic space of the house, and made measurements everywhere, so that not one inch should be unaccounted for. Among other things, he found that the height of the building was seventy-four feet, but on adding together the heights of all the separate rooms, and making every allowance for the space between, which he ascertained by borings,
> 10 he could not bring the total to more than seventy feet. There were four feet unaccounted for. These could only be at the top of the building. He knocked a hole, therefore, in the lath-and-plaster ceiling of the highest room, and there, sure enough, he came upon another little garret above it, which had been sealed up and was known to no one. In the centre stood the treasure-chest, resting
> 15 upon two rafters. He lowered it through the hole, and there it lies. He computes the value of the jewels at not less than half a million sterling.'
>
> At the mention of this gigantic sum we all stared at one another open-eyed. Miss Morstan, could we secure her rights, would change from a needy governess to the richest heiress in England. Surely it was the place of a loyal
> 20 friend to rejoice at such news; yet I am ashamed to say that selfishness took me by the soul, and that my heart turned as heavy as lead within me. I stammered out some few halting words of congratulation, and then sat downcast, with my head drooped, deaf to the babble of our new acquaintance.

4. Starting with this extract, explore how Conan Doyle presents different attitudes to wealth in the novel. Write about:

- how different attitudes to wealth are presented in the extract
- how different attitudes to wealth are presented in the novel as a whole.

[30 marks]

NOW read this further theme question

Read this extract from Chapter 8 in which Holmes and Watson are travelling back in the morning to Baker Street after working all night on the murder case. Then answer the question that follows.

> We pulled up at the Great Peter Street post-office, and Holmes despatched his wire. 'Whom do you think that is to?' he asked, as we resumed our journey.
>
> 'I am sure I don't know.'
>
> 'You remember the Baker Street division of the detective police force whom I
> 5 employed in the Jefferson Hope case?'
>
> 'Well,' said I, laughing.
>
> 'This is just the case where they might be invaluable. If they fail, I have other resources; but I shall try them first. That wire was to my dirty little lieutenant, Wiggins, and I expect that he and his gang will be with us before we have finished
> 10 our breakfast.'
>
> It was between eight and nine o'clock now, and I was conscious of a strong reaction after the successive excitements of the night. I was limp and weary, befogged in mind and fatigued in body. I had not the professional enthusiasm which carried my companion on, nor could I look at the matter as a mere abstract
> 15 intellectual problem. As far as the death of Bartholomew Sholto went, I had heard little good of him, and could feel no intense antipathy to his murderers. The treasure, however, was a different matter. That, or part of it, belonged rightfully to Miss Morstan. While there was a chance of recovering it I was ready to devote my life to the one object. True, if I found it it would probably put her forever beyond
> 20 my reach. Yet it would be a petty and selfish love which would be influenced by such a thought as that. If Holmes could work to find the criminals, I had a tenfold stronger reason to urge me on to find the treasure.
>
> A bath at Baker Street and a complete change freshened me up wonderfully. When I came down to our room I found the breakfast laid and Holmes pouring
> 25 out the coffee.
>
> 'Here it is,' said he, laughing, and pointing to an open newspaper. 'The energetic Jones and the ubiquitous reporter have fixed it up between them. But you have had enough of the case. Better have your ham and eggs first.'

5. Starting with this extract, explore how Conan Doyle presents love and friendship. Write about:

- how Conan Doyle presents love and friendship in this extract
- how Conan Doyle presents love and friendship in the novel as a whole.

[30 marks]

EXAM PRACTICE Planning your theme response

Five key stages to follow

1. **Read** the **question**; **highlight** key words.
2. **Read** the **passage** with the **key words** from the **question** in mind.
3. Quickly **generate ideas** for your response.
4. **Plan** for paragraphs.
5. **Write** your response; **check it** against your plan as you progress.

What do I focus on?

Highlight the **key words**:

> 4. Starting with this extract, explore how Conan Doyle presents different attitudes to wealth in the novel. Write about:
>   - how different attitudes to wealth are presented in the extract
>   - how different attitudes to wealth are presented in the novel as a whole.
>
> **[30 marks]**

What do they tell you? Focus on both the extract and whole text; explain what specific methods Conan Doyle uses; stick to wealth as the main topic.

How should I read the passage?

- Check for any immediate links to the question (e.g. Bartholomew's search for the treasure).
- Look for any evidence/quotations you could highlight (e.g. treasure's hiding place **'sealed up and was known to no one'**).

How do I get my ideas?

Note your ideas in a spider diagram or list them in a table:

The extract

Bartholomew's desperation to find treasure, 'made measurements everywhere'

Major Sholto's hiding of the treasure, 'sealed up'

Watson fears Mary becoming 'richest heiress', is downcast, gives 'halting congratulations'

How wealth is presented

The novel as a whole

Holmes says 'the work is my highest reward'

Watson fears being 'vulgar fortune-seeker'

74

The extract	The novel as a whole
• Bartholomew desperate to find treasure, 'made measurements everywhere'	• Holmes says 'highest reward' is work, not money
• Major Sholto hides the treasure, 'sealed up'	• Watson fears Mary will think him 'vulgar fortune-seeker'
• Watson fears Mary becoming 'richest heiress'	
• Watson's 'downcast' congratulations to Mary	

How do I structure my ideas?

Make a **plan** for **paragraphs**.* Decide the order for your points:

- Paragraph 1: Go straight into your first point: *Bartholomew's desperate search for the treasure.*
- Paragraph 2: *Treasure hidden by Major Sholto – context of Indian Mutiny.*
- Paragraph 3: *Watson fears Mary will become the 'richest heiress' and that wealth will come between them.*
- Paragraph 4: *Holmes's attitude to wealth – work 'highest reward'.*
- Paragraph 5: *Watson fears Mary will think him a 'vulgar fortune-seeker'.*

How do I write effectively?

Write **clear**, **analytical** paragraphs and **embed** your evidence fluently, e.g.

Conan Doyle presents different attitudes to wealth in the novel. In the extract Thaddeus explains the great efforts made by his brother, Bartholomew, to find the hidden treasure-chest. Bartholomew made precise 'measurements everywhere' and carefully 'worked out' the location. The word 'everywhere' emphasises his desperation. Conan Doyle later contrasts Bartholomew's frantic desire for personal wealth with other characters' determination to see the wealth shared more fairly.

- Overview
- Focus on extract
- Quotations embedded in sentence
- Analysis of language
- Summary point linking to rest of novel

Now you try!

Re-read Question 5 on page 73 and plan your response in the same way.

* The plan above and the sample answers on pages 76 and 78 have five paragraphs, but you don't need to be limited to this if you have more points to include (and time to write them!).

What does a Grade 5 answer look like?

Read the task again, then the sample answer below.

4. Starting with this extract, explore how Conan Doyle presents different attitudes to wealth in the novel. Write about:

- how different attitudes to wealth are presented in the extract
- how different attitudes to wealth are presented in the novel as a whole.

[30 marks]

In the passage Thaddeus Sholto first describes his brother Bartholomew's search for the Agra treasure hidden at Pondicherry Lodge. Conan Doyle shows that Bartholomew went to great lengths to find the treasure hidden by his father as he carefully studied the house and 'worked out' where it was hidden. Thaddeus describes in detail the way the hiding place was found by Bartholomew's 'measurements' and this shows how desperate his brother was to get the treasure for himself.

AO1 Clear statement with reference to structure of extract

AO2 Close reference to word use and what it means

Although his name is not mentioned in the passage it is clear that their father, Major Sholto, had carefully hidden the treasure in the 'highest room' and had 'sealed up' the entrance. This shows that Major Sholto was worried that his treasure, which he took when he betrayed Jonathan Small and the rest of the 'Four', would be found by them. Major Sholto's fearful attitude to this wealth may reflect the fact that it was stolen during the Indian Mutiny. This shows that he was worried that it did not really belong to him anyway and could possibly be taken from him at any time.

AO3 A point of context

In the passage Conan Doyle contrasts this with the behaviour of Dr Watson who learns of the 'gigantic sum' the treasure is valued at. His first thought is about Mary, changing her from a 'needy governess' to the 'richest heiress'. He congratulates her but still has worries about his lack of money and poor health. Watson's worries about whether or not he would be a suitable future husband for Mary have troubled him since his very first meeting with her in Chapter 2.

AO2 Link made between different characters

AO2 Relevant idea but not developed sufficiently

AO2 Link not fully explained

In contrast Conan Doyle shows Holmes earlier in the novel to be a character who does not appear to be concerned with money. When Holmes describes his detective work to Watson in the opening chapter he says that the pleasure he gets from it is his 'highest reward'. In this way, Conan Doyle suggests that Holmes is only motivated by work and this sets him apart from many of the other characters in the novel such as Bartholomew Sholto, Major Sholto and the Four who are driven by their desire for wealth.

— Paragraph 4

Overall Bartholomew and Dr Watson are both presented here as concerned by wealth but for different reasons. Elsewhere in the novel we see Jonathan Small's obsession with wealth and the treasure. First he desires wealth to improve his life because he describes himself as a 'useless cripple'. He is 'useless' because in Victorian times the poor and disabled were not supported and life would have been very harsh for him without money. Later Small's attitude to wealth is that it represents justice for the Four and 'vengeance' against Major Sholto who betrayed them.

— Paragraph 5

Check the skills

Re-read paragraphs four and five of this response and:

- highlight other **points** made
- circle any reference to **context**
- underline any places where the student has made an **interpretation**.

Now you try!

Look again at paragraph three ('*In the passage Conan Doyle contrasts …*') and improve it by:

- **Explaining** why the phrases 'needy governess' and 'richest heiress' are significant
- Adding a **reference or quotation** about Watson from Chapter 2 to support the point about Watson's early worries about his income and health
- Ending with a **summary point** about how the treasure is presented as a barrier to Watson and Mary here and in the rest of the novel
- Improving the overall **style** by making sure your sentences **flow**; using **connectives** to **link** ideas

What does a Grade 7+ answer look like?

Read the task again, then the sample answer below.

4. Starting with this extract, explore how Conan Doyle presents different attitudes to wealth in the novel. Write about:
   - how different attitudes to wealth are presented in the extract
   - how different attitudes to wealth are presented in the novel as a whole. **[30 marks]**

Conan Doyle presents many different attitudes to wealth yet the most powerful impact is made by the contrast in the novel between the corrupting desire to possess wealth with the selfless rejection of wealth for moral reasons. In this passage Conan Doyle contrasts Bartholomew Sholto's desperate attempts to find the treasure his father has hidden with Dr Watson's feelings that wealth will be a 'golden barrier' to his hopes for a relationship with Mary Morstan.

> **AO1** Clear statement sets out argument

> **AO2** Immediate structural link made with evidence to earlier part of novel

Bartholomew's efforts to find the treasure are portrayed in this passage as a frantic, obsessive search. Thaddeus tells Holmes and Watson that his brother 'worked out' the 'measurements' of the house to find where the treasure had been hidden. This reveals how his search becomes a mathematical problem which strangely mirrors Holmes's own precise scientific methods in solving crime. Yet, ultimately it emphasises the contrast between them as Holmes earlier stated that his investigative work alone is his 'highest reward'.

> **AO1** Very well expressed point

> **AO2** Perceptive interpretation

> **AO2** Structural link to earlier part of novel

Bartholomew's desire for personal wealth reflects Major Sholto's attitude to the treasure. This is made clear by Thaddeus who states earlier that Bartholomew shared his 'father's fault' of 'cursed greed'. Major Sholto's 'greed' is shown in this extract when the hiding place is described by Conan Doyle as 'sealed up and known to no one'. The verb phrase 'sealed up' not only indicates Major Sholto's desire to keep the treasure for himself, but also implies his fears that it might be taken from him. This could symbolise how this stolen treasure is almost supernaturally 'cursed' as it was taken unlawfully during the Indian Mutiny: an example of how Victorian ruling classes could exploit the wealth of the British Empire.

> **AO2** Perceptive analysis of language

> **AO2** Point is developed and interpreted

> **AO3** Excellent understanding of context

Watson, however, views the treasure as a 'golden barrier' between him and Mary. In the passage Watson says 'selfishness took me by the soul' and the religious noun 'soul' reflects his strong sense of morality regarding wealth. Dr Watson's attitude reflects a rigid Victorian attitude to wealth and social class. If Mary Morstan became the 'richest heiress', then Watson, a poorly paid army doctor, would not be considered a suitable marriage partner.

Finally, although he is presented as the criminal, Jonathan Small's attitude to wealth in my view could be linked with Watson's as he also views the treasure in moral terms. Small's version of morality, however, is a corrupted one. In the spirit of justice and fairness, he is determined that others receive their share. At the end of the novel Small says 'it's been the sign of the four with us always' and this is a symbol of his loyalty, rather than individual greed. When Small throws the treasure in the Thames it suggests that no one deserves this looted wealth and by concluding the novel with Watson's engagement, Conan Doyle emphasises the importance of love over wealth.

Paragraph 4

Paragraph 5

Check the skills

Re-read paragraphs four and five of this response and:

- identify any particularly **fluent** or **well-expressed** ideas
- find any further references to **context**
- highlight any places where the student has shown **deeper insight** and offered **original** or particularly **thoughtful** ideas or made interesting **links**.

Now you try!

Now, using the plan you made for Question 5 on page 75, write a full response. Here's a reminder of the question:

5. Starting with this extract, explore how Conan Doyle presents love and friendship. Write about:

   - how Conan Doyle presents love and friendship in this extract
   - how Conan Doyle presents love and friendship in the novel as a whole. **[30 marks]**

Try to match your answer to the High Level objectives on page 63.

Now you try!

Now, practise applying the skills you have learned to these **two new questions**. In each case:

- Note down key points from the extract.
- Select the key quotations you want to use from the extract.
- Repeat the process with other ideas from the novel as a whole.
- Write your answer.
- Look at the suggested list of key points you could have made for each question in the **Answers** (page 88).

Read this extract from Chapter 11 in which Watson takes the iron treasure-box to Mary Morstan's lodgings. Then answer the question that follows.

> She was seated by the open window, dressed in some sort of white diaphanous material, with a little touch of scarlet at the neck and waist. The soft light of a shaded lamp fell upon her as she leaned back in the basket chair, playing over her sweet, grave face, and tinting with a dull, metallic sparkle the rich coils of her
> 5 luxuriant hair. One white arm and hand drooped over the side of the chair, and her whole pose and figure spoke of an absorbing melancholy. At the sound of my foot-fall she sprang to her feet, however, and a bright flush of surprise and of pleasure colored her pale cheeks.
>   'I heard a cab drive up,' she said. 'I thought that Mrs. Forrester had come back
> 10 very early, but I never dreamed that it might be you. What news have you brought me?'
>   'I have brought something better than news,' said I, putting down the box upon the table and speaking jovially and boisterously, though my heart was heavy within me. 'I have brought you something which is worth all the news in the world. I have
> 15 brought you a fortune.'
>   She glanced at the iron box. 'Is that the treasure, then?' she asked, coolly enough.
>   'Yes, this is the great Agra treasure. Half of it is yours and half is Thaddeus Sholto's. You will have a couple of hundred thousand each. Think of that! An annuity of ten thousand pounds. There will be few richer young ladies in England.
> 20 Is it not glorious?'
>   I think that I must have been rather overacting my delight, and that she detected a hollow ring in my congratulations, for I saw her eyebrows rise a little, and she glanced at me curiously.
>   'If I have it,' said she, 'I owe it to you.'

6. Starting with this extract, explore how Conan Doyle presents Mary Morstan. Write about:

- how Conan Doyle presents Mary Morstan in this extract
- how Conan Doyle presents Mary Morstan in the novel as a whole.

[30 marks]

Read this extract from Chapter 10 in which Watson is describing the river chase to catch the criminals Jonathan Small and Tonga. Then answer the question that follows.

> I have coursed many creatures in many countries during my checkered career, but never did sport give me such a wild thrill as this mad, flying man-hunt down the Thames. Steadily we drew in upon them, yard by yard. In the silence of the night we could hear the panting and clanking of their machinery. The man in the
> 5 stern still crouched upon the deck, and his arms were moving as though he were busy, while every now and then he would look up and measure with a glance the distance which still separated us. Nearer we came and nearer. Jones yelled to them to stop. We were not more than four boat's lengths behind them, both boats flying at a tremendous pace. It was a clear reach of the river, with Barking Level upon
> 10 one side and the melancholy Plumstead Marshes upon the other. At our hail the man in the stern sprang up from the deck and shook his two clinched fists at us, cursing the while in a high, cracked voice. He was a good-sized, powerful man, and as he stood poising himself with legs astride I could see that from the thigh downwards there was but a wooden stump upon the right side. At the sound of his
> 15 strident, angry cries there was movement in the huddled bundle upon the deck. It straightened itself into a little black man–the smallest I have ever seen–with a great, misshapen head and a shock of tangled, dishevelled hair. Holmes had already drawn his revolver, and I whipped out mine at the sight of this savage, distorted creature. He was wrapped in some sort of dark ulster or blanket, which left only his
> 20 face exposed; but that face was enough to give a man a sleepless night. Never have I seen features so deeply marked with all bestiality and cruelty. His small eyes glowed and burned with a sombre light, and his thick lips were writhed back from his teeth, which grinned and chattered at us with a half animal fury.
> 'Fire if he raises his hand,' said Holmes, quietly. We were within a boat's-length
> 25 by this time, and almost within touch of our quarry.

7. Starting with this extract, explore how Conan Doyle creates dramatic action. Write about:

- how Conan Doyle creates dramatic action in this extract
- how Conan Doyle creates dramatic action in the novel as a whole.

[30 marks]

81

GLOSSARY

Literary terms	Explanation
adjective	a word used to describe something or somebody (e.g. the red hat)
adverb	used to modify a verb, adjective or another adverb, sometimes formed by adding 'ly' to an adjective
alliteration	where the same sound is repeated in a stretch of language, usually at the beginning of words
anti-climax	a disappointing end to an exciting series of events in a story
character	an individual in a work of fiction
chronology	the order of the events of a story in time
climax	the highpoint of a play, act or story
context	events, issues or concerns which are happening outside the world of the story, i.e. in the real world
counterpoint	a person or object which provides a significant contrast to another
crime story	a story in which the solving of a crime is a central feature
detective story	a story in which a detective tries to solve a crime
dialect	accent and vocabulary, varying by region and social background
dialogue	speech and conversation between characters
first-person	a story told using the pronoun 'I'
flashback	a scene or part of a play, novel or film that goes back in time, prior to the main story
foreboding	a sense that something bad is about to happen
form	the type of text the writer is creating (e.g. a letter, novel or short story)
frame narrator	a fictional character who narrates a frame story
Gothic	in literature a style that includes horror, the supernatural or eerie, romance and death
imagery	descriptive language that uses images to make actions, objects and characters more vivid in the reader's mind
imperative	a sentence which gives a command
juxtapose	to put side-by-side to create a contrasting effect
metaphor	when one thing is used to describe another to create a striking or unusual image
mood	the tone or atmosphere created by an artistic work

Literary terms	Explanation
motif	a repeated image or symbol
narrator	the voice or person that tells the story
noun	a word that denotes an object
novel	a fictional narrative of length
onomatopoeia	a word that suggests its meaning through its sound (e.g. 'meow', 'squelch')
pace	the speed at which events occur or are recounted in a story
pathetic fallacy	a technique that suggests weather is reflecting a character's mood
personification	the treatment or description of an object or idea as though it is human with human feelings and attributes
plosive alliteration	where the same plosive sound (usually p or b) is used in a stretch of language, often at the beginning of words
plot	the main events in a novel
resolution	the end of a story that ties its different elements together
rhetorical question	a question where no answer is expected or where the answer is so obvious that it does not need to be stated
romance	a story that has a love relationship as its main focus
setting	the place and time where the action of a story takes place
simile	when one thing is compared directly with another using 'like' or 'as'
slang	very informal language
stereotype	a fixed or simplified version of a type of person
subplot	a secondary storyline that supports the main one, often by reinforcing a theme
suspense	when the reader is uncertain, uneasy or anxious about what will happen next in a story
symbol	something that represents something else, usually with meanings that are widely known (e.g. a dove as a symbol of peace)
theme	an idea running through a work of literature or art
tone	see mood
topic sentence	a sentence that expresses the main idea of a paragraph, sometimes the first of the paragraph
verb	a word that denotes an action (e.g. he laughed suddenly)
vocabulary	the choice of words used by a writer

ANSWERS

Note that the sample paragraphs given here provide only one possible approach to each task. Many other approaches would also be valid and appropriate.

PLOT AND STRUCTURE

Chapters 1 and 2 – Now you try! (page 7)

The opening chapter introduces Holmes, and the reader's first impression is that he has a very logical and unemotional attitude to each client. This is shown by his statement that each one is 'a mere unit, a factor in a problem'. Holmes's use of the words 'unit' and 'factor' here shows his cold, almost scientific, mathematical approach to people.

Chapters 3 and 4 – Now you try! (page 9)

In the mysterious London night-time setting, Conan Doyle describes the city as having 'monster tentacles' and the use of this image creates the effect of a dark, menacing presence. The 'giant city' is therefore presented as huge and dangerous. This Gothic 'monster' imagery adds to the sense of Victorian London as a setting for uncontrolled criminal activity and it creates fear and anticipation in the reader.

Chapters 5 and 6 – Now you try! (page 11)

The theme of friendship is explored in Chapter 6 through the close working relationship between the characters of Holmes and Watson. When Holmes says to Watson 'You know my methods. Apply them', this shows familiarity between them as Holmes begins with 'My dear Watson' to soften his rather direct remarks. Holmes's command to 'apply' his methods here also reflects the instructional nature of their friendship which, in other parts of the novel, resembles a pupil and teacher relationship.

Chapters 7–9 – Now you try! (page 13)

In Chapter 7 there is a contrast between different settings with Watson's description of the house of Mrs Forrester as 'a tranquil English home' and the 'wild, dark business' of the criminal world. The juxtaposition of the adjectives 'tranquil' with 'wild' and 'dark' emphasises the Victorian ideal of home as a safe, feminine sanctuary from dangerous city life.

Chapter 10 – Now you try! (page 15)

The crime story form is apparent when Watson says that no 'sport' had ever given him such a 'thrill' as 'this mad, flying man-hunt down the Thames' and Conan Doyles's use of language signals to the reader that this will be the exciting climax of the story. His description of the 'man-hunt' as 'mad' and 'flying' suggests an adventure story, almost like Victorian big-game hunting, which contrasts with the earlier romantic subplot.

Chapter 11 – Now you try! (page 17)

The theme of love is apparent when Watson states that 'Whoever had lost a treasure, I knew that night that I had gained one.' His use of the metaphor of the 'treasure' to refer to Mary's love and her acceptance of his marriage proposal shows the high value that Watson places upon human relationships. This contrasts with other characters, such as Major Sholto, who instead show selfishness and greed.

Chapter 12 – Now you try! (page 19)

The structure of the novel includes other stories: for example, when Abdullah Khan invites the reader to 'Hearken, then, to what I have to say.' The effect is to signal that a different narrator is taking over and that we must follow what he has 'to say'. The use of different narrators within Watson's overall frame narrative, such as Thaddeus Sholto's and Mary Morstan's, helps introduce important flashbacks into the story.

Form and structure – Now you try! (page 21)

Gothic elements, which heighten tension, are revealed in the description of the discovery of Bartholomew Sholto's body with the 'moonlight streaming into the room'. The reference to 'moonlight' and to Bartholomew's face which 'hung' above them creates an almost supernatural image and ghostly atmosphere and suggests that dark criminal forces are at work. Earlier descriptions of the city evoke the same atmosphere of darkness and danger.

Quick revision – Quick quiz (pages 22–3)

1. Watson's brother. 2. Six, once a year. 3. Four linked crosses. 4. Wearing a yellow turban and loose white robes. 5. Asks him to examine his heart. 6. Pondicherry Lodge. 7. Brown stick and thorn. 8. Murder suspect. 9. Mark of a wooden stump. 10. Athelney Jones. 11. Toby the dog. 12. Baker Street Irregulars. 13. Thaddeus Sholto. 14. Jacobson's Yard. 15. Gets stuck in mud. 16. It's empty. 17. Delighted. 18. Indian Mutiny. 19. Achmet. 20. Watson's and Mary's engagement.

Quick revision – Power paragraphs (page 23)

1. Holmes is presented as a very logical character in the opening chapter. This is shown when he states that detection ought to be 'an exact science'. His use of the noun 'science' shows that he views his work in a different way to others, such as Watson, who engages with the cases more personally. Holmes says his work should be 'cold and unemotional' and these two adjectives apply equally to his methods and to his character.

2. Watson's reaction to the loss of the Agra treasure in Chapter 11 reflects his view that such incredible wealth could only act as a 'barrier' between him and Mary. At first he disguises his feelings when the empty iron-box is revealed, but when Mary reveals her own relief Watson can finally express his love. The 'lost' treasure no longer matters and Watson's assertion that he has 'gained' his own treasure celebrates the triumph of love over wealth.

Quick revision – Exam practice (page 23)

*   When Watson hands the watch to Holmes he thinks that the test he is setting him is 'an impossible one' but then Holmes starts to look in detail at the watch with 'a powerful convex lens'. The use of the lens shows Holmes's powers of precise observation and even though he says he does not have enough 'data' he is able to draw very detailed conclusions. Holmes is able to deduce that the watch belonged to Watson's brother and that he had a drink problem.

*   Watson is initially offended by Holmes's manner and findings, shown by the fact that he 'sprang' from his chair thinking that Holmes had cheated. Then Holmes goes

through his observations of the 'thousands of scratches' which mark a 'drunkard's watch' and his use of this precise language forces Watson to admit he should have had 'more faith' in Holmes. This shows the mutual respect which lies at the heart of their friendship.

SETTING AND CONTEXT

Victorian Britain – Now you try! (page 25)

Victorian attitudes to race are reflected when Watson describes Tonga during the river chase as 'this savage, distorted creature'. The use of the adjective 'savage' shows that Victorians often viewed non-white races as uncivilised and saw unfamiliar behaviour and customs as barbaric. Describing Tonga as a 'distorted creature' also suggests he is animal-like and less than human which further emphasises this judgemental view.

Colonialism and empire – Now you try! (page 27)

Jonathan Small's praise for Tonga's sense of duty is shown by his description of him as 'devoted' and as someone who 'would do anything to serve me'. Although Tonga's devotion and loyalty to Small are in return for being saved by him, Conan Doyle's use of the verb 'serve' here reflects Victorian attitudes to people of the British Empire who were often exploited as servants to members of a white ruling class.

Quick revision – Quick quiz (page 29)

1. Baker Street Irregulars. 2. Tonga. 3. Officers of the law/ police. 4. Mary Morstan. 5. Mud-banks on River Thames. 6. Agra. 7. Baker Street. 8. Tonga. 9. Major Sholto. 10. Indian Mutiny.

Quick revision – Power paragraphs (page 29)

- The interior setting of Thaddeus's home emphasises how exotic treasures from the countries in the empire were brought back to Britain and displayed, almost as trophies by the wealthy. Conan Doyle contrasts the outside of Thaddeus's suburban house with its contents of 'tiger-skins' and items of 'Eastern luxury'. This is emphasised by the size of the 'huge hookah', an oriental tobacco pipe, which seems very out of place in this English home.
- This stark contrast of East and West in his home is presented initially as an expression of Thaddeus's eccentric character, but in fact also suggests that his trophies, like the Agra treasure, do not belong in London.

CHARACTERS

Sherlock Holmes – Now you try! (page 31)

Holmes's keen interest in the latest scientific methods is revealed by Conan Doyle when Watson states in Chapter 9 that, during a break in the case, Holmes occupied himself with 'abstruse chemical analysis' and 'heating of retorts and distilling of vapors'. References to precise scientific processes such as 'distilling' and to laboratory equipment such as 'retorts' reflect Holmes's logical character along with a growing Victorian interest in the potential of scientific analysis.

Dr Watson – Now you try! (page 33)

Watson's sense of care and responsibility for Holmes is revealed by Conan Doyle when Watson comments on

Holmes's drug use and warns that this could result in 'tissue change' and, more seriously, 'permanent weakness'. The reference to 'weakness', and the destruction of Holmes's powers, shows Dr Watson's deep concern for his friend and his use of precise medical terms reflects his understanding that Holmes will respond only to science, not emotion.

Miss Morstan – Now you try! (page 35)

At the end, Conan Doyle uses Mary's character to explore the theme of wealth through her reaction to the opening of the iron box. When it is opened and found to be empty, she 'calmly' comments, 'The treasure is lost'. Conan Doyle's use of the adverb 'calmly' and her simple, unemotional statement about the loss reveals that ultimately she is a character motivated by love, not wealth.

Thaddeus Sholto – Now you try! (page 37)

Conan Doyle contrasts Thaddeus's caring nature with his twin brother's unfeeling nature when Thaddeus argues with Bartholomew about the division of the treasure and pleads that Mary be sent 'a detached pearl at fixed intervals' so that she may never be 'destitute'. The use of the adjective 'destitute' is emotive and shows Thaddeus's concern and even feeling of guilt. His actions therefore act in counterpoint to his brother's greed and self-interest.

Jonathan Small – Now you try! (page 39)

The contradictions in Small's character are shown when Watson comments on first meeting him that there was 'more sorrow than anger' in his expression. Conan Doyle's use of the noun 'sorrow' reflects Small's sadness about the betrayal of the Four and the injustices of his life and it is this emotion, rather than the 'anger' which we might expect from a hardened criminal, that Watson notices.

Athelney Jones – Now you try! (page 41)

Conan Doyle reveals the contrast between Jones and Holmes, when Jones says to Holmes 'we all know that you are a connoisseur of crime, but duty is duty', using elevated language when comparing Holmes's attitude to his own. He chooses the noun 'connoisseur' to suggest someone who prefers the exciting and unusual criminal cases rather than the daily routine and 'duty' of police work.

Minor characters – Now you try! (page 43)

Conan Doyle explores the theme of wealth through Bartholomew Sholto's character when his brother Thaddeus says that the suggestion of sending pearls to help Mary caused an argument between them. Thaddeus states that the pearls 'were evidently of great value' and because of this his brother was 'averse to part with them'. The worth of the pearls is clear from the adjective 'great' and Bartholomew's desire to keep all the treasure reveals his greed and corruption.

Quick revision – Quick quiz (pages 44–5)

1. A Study in Scarlet. 2. Holmes, about the police. 3. Mary Morstan. 4. Dr Watson. 5. Thaddeus Sholto. 6. Death of her father. 7. Bartholomew Sholto. 8. Thaddeus's. 9. Bartholomew Sholto, poisoned dart. 10. Jonathan Small. 11. Inheritance of the treasure. 12. Andaman Islands. 13. Thaddeus Sholto. 14. Sherlock Holmes. 15. Major Sholto. 16. Small, with wooden leg. 17. Mary's hand in marriage. 18. Mohammet Singh. 19. Small on Tonga. 20. Sherlock Holmes.

Quick revision – Power paragraphs (page 45)

1. The Sholto twins are used by Conan Doyle to explore the theme of duality. Thaddeus, in some ways, is kinder: he feels concerned that Mary could be 'destitute' if the treasure is not shared and his views are contrasted with Bartholomew's heavily guarded home at Pondicherry Lodge and his plan to find and keep the treasure for himself. The twins are opposites – good and bad – and reflect Victorian interest in dual personalities.
2. Conan Doyle shows that the treasure is a barrier to the romantic relationship between Watson and Mary with Watson's concerns that Mary might see him as 'a mere vulgar fortune-seeker'. Given that many characters in the novel are presented as 'fortune seekers', motivated entirely by wealth, Watson's decision to wait until the treasure is lost to propose to Mary shows the reader that it is love, not money, which is his ultimate prize.

Quick revision – Exam practice (page 45)

- The contrasting way the characters respond to this lack of activity is used by Conan Doyle to reflect the differences between them. Whereas Watson awakes after a night's sleep 'strengthened and refreshed', Holmes has clearly been awake all night and appears 'dark and troubled'. The contrasting paired adjectives here show that Watson can detach himself from work whereas Holmes is entirely preoccupied and 'troubled' by the case.
- Differences are also shown by what each character does next. Holmes insists that he must 'remain on guard' whereas Watson's intends to go to Mrs Forrester's to see Mary and give her the latest news. Holmes then warns that 'women are never entirely to be trusted' and Conan Doyle's use of the general plural noun 'women' emphasises Holmes's suspicious and cynical nature. In contrast, Watson's outrage at this 'atrocious' remark shows him to be more tolerant and trusting, both in his attitude to women and to other people in general.

THEMES

Crime and justice – Now you try! (page 47)

The Sign of the Four itself symbolises the theme of justice, as is shown in Chapter 7 when Holmes suggests that Small's leaving the symbol on Bartholomew Sholto's body made the crime not a 'common murder' but instead 'an act of justice'. This judgement becomes much clearer in the final chapters of the novel where Small admits that he was motivated by revenge against Major Sholto and a sense of burning injustice against him and his associates.

Love and friendship – Now you try! (page 49)

The teacher–student relationship between Holmes and Watson is clearly shown by Conan Doyle describing Holmes as having 'the air of a clinical professor expounding to his class'. This suggests their relationship is like that of a teacher and his apprentice. The choice of 'expounding' also shows Holmes's assumption that he can train Watson. Watson is in awe of Holmes's knowledge, but the verb 'expounding' is slightly critical and therefore shows that he sometimes resents being treated as a student.

Wealth – Now you try! (page 51)

Major Sholto shows how corrupted he is by wealth when he admits that he was a victim of 'cursed greed' and that this was his 'besetting sin through life'. Conan Doyle's use of the adjective 'cursed' and the noun 'sin' are religious in their connotations and provide a moral tone for the reader which guides them to judge Major Sholto's actions more harshly.

Duality – Now you try! (page 53)

The duality of Holmes and Watson is shown by the way Holmes reacts in a cold, professional way to the arrival of Mary Morstan. He says that 'emotional qualities are antagonistic to clear reasoning' as a criticism of Watson's warm, heartfelt response to her. Conan Doyle's contrast between emotion and reason here, revealed through his two main characters, presents them as opposites and reflects a Victorian interest in opposing personalities or duality.

Science – Now you try! (page 55)

The description of Bartholomew Sholto's home laboratory as 'littered over with Bunsen burners, test-tubes, and retorts' reflects the increasing popularity of science as a hobby in the Victorian period. Conan Doyle's listing and references to specific scientific equipment, such as Bunsen burners, presents Bartholomew's laboratory as well-equipped. This therefore reveals scientific analysis as a new leisure activity for wealthy, educated men.

Quick revision – Quick quiz (pages 56–7)

1. Agra treasure. 2. Student. 3. Sherlock Holmes and Bartholomew Sholto. 4. Saved his life. 5. Sharing treasure with Mary. 6. Andaman Islands. 7. Baker Street Irregulars. 8. Dr Watson. 9. Tonga. 10. Bartholomew. 11. Opposite characteristics. 12. Jonathan Small. 13. Thrown in the Thames. 14. Sherlock Holmes. 15. Pearls. 16. Tonga. 17. Holmes. 18. Bangs head on treasure chest. 19. Beats him with wooden leg. 20. Watson.

Quick revision – Power paragraphs (page 57)

1. Jonathan Small seeks the lost treasure mainly out of a sense of justice. Conan Doyle shows this when Small says that he would rather live in a 'convict's cell' than see someone else live 'at ease in a palace' with the money which should be his. The stark contrast between the nouns 'cell' and 'palace' emphasises Small's obsession with fairness and shows his attitude to wealth is less about greed than justice for the Four.
2. Conan Doyle uses scientific terms and concepts to show that Holmes is a new type of detective with a rational, logical approach to solving crime. This is shown when Holmes says to Watson 'Individuals vary but percentages remain constant' when they are discussing criminal behaviour before the river chase. Holmes's faith in 'percentages' which do not change, or stay 'constant', shows that his interest in people is scientific, rather than emotional or 'individual', unlike Watson's.

Quick revision – Exam practice (page 57)

- Conan Doyle uses language to emphasise the violence of the murder of Achmet and also the darker nature of Jonathan Small. When Small recounts his meeting with the merchant, the description of Achmet makes him seem very vulnerable. Small describes his 'fat frightened face' and when he eventually fires at him he falls 'like a shot rabbit'. The 'f' alliteration and the simile in which Achmet is a hunted animal emphasise his helplessness.
- Jonathan Small is brutally honest about his actions and

says that although his heart 'softened' to Achmet the 'thought of his treasure' made him 'hard and bitter'. The contrast between these adjectives shows how Small's 'soft' sympathetic feelings struggle against his 'hard and bitter' desire for the treasure. This is used by Conan Doyle to show the violence of this murder and the duality of Small's character, later revealed in his loyalty to Tonga.

LANGUAGE

Imagery and vocabulary – Now you try! (page 59)

Mr Sherman is effectively characterised, through Conan Doyle's use of dialogue, when he threatens Holmes, saying 'I have a wiper in the bag, an' I'll drop it on your 'ead'. Conan Doyle's use of the Cockney dialect pronunciation of words such as 'viper' and 'head' reveal that he is a slightly comic, lower-class character and part of a London underworld which Holmes uses to help his investigations.

Quick Revision – Quick quiz (page 61)

1. Metaphor. 2. Motif. 3. Use of specialist scientific terms. 4. Mysterious. 5. Lower class. 6. Romance. 7. Frame narrator. 8. Jonathan Small's story/newspaper reports/Mary's story/Thaddeus Sholto's story. 9. Chronology. 10. Flashback.

Quick revision – Power paragraphs (page 61)

1. Conan Doyle's description of the journey to Thaddeus Sholto's house in Chapter 3 creates an eerie impression of night-time London. The city is described as having 'monster tentacles' being thrown out into the country, and this metaphor and the use of the noun 'tentacles' makes the city seem like a living creature ready to grab and attack. This image and the use of darkness here creates a Gothic, almost supernatural, atmosphere.

2. The river chase in Chapter 10 is a dramatic end to the criminal investigation and this is emphasised by Watson's description of his own 'wild thrill' of the chase which he calls 'a mad, flying man-hunt down the Thames'. The use of the highly active adjectives 'wild', 'mad' and 'flying' makes the reader share Watson's sense of excitement and anticipation so that when the criminals are caught it becomes an effective, exciting climax to the story.

EXAM PRACTICE

Planning your character response – Now you try! (page 67)

- **Paragraph 1**: Small's anger at Major Sholto is shown by his use of names 'villain' and 'scoundrel' because of Sholto's theft of the treasure.
- **Paragraph 2**: The desire for 'vengeance' becomes a dangerous, all-consuming 'passion' and Small does not care about punishment – the 'law' or the 'gallows'.
- **Paragraph 3**: Small's thoughts become increasingly violent – wants to have 'his hand on his throat' and his thoughts about the treasure now a 'smaller thing' than 'slaying of Sholto'.
- **Paragraph 4**: Small's care for the 'little Andaman Islander' shows his caring side. He nurses him over 'a couple of months' and saves his life. Also clear in Chapter 12 where he calls him 'faithful mate'.

- **Paragraph 5**: This caring side is shown by his decision to learn some of Tonga's 'lingo' which is evidence of how much this friendship meant to him. Also his loyalty to the rest of the Four: in Chapter 12 he states, 'it was the sign of the four with us always'.

Grade 5+ sample answer – Check the skills (page 69)

- **Points**: Earlier in the novel, when Thaddeus meets Mary, his behaviour is unusual in that he tells her suddenly about his father's death without thinking about how this shocking news will affect her. He also is more concerned with his own health and asks Dr Watson about his symptoms. Thaddeus's attitude to the treasure in the rest of the novel is also shown to be unusual compared to other characters.
- **Context**: Conan Doyle is saying to the reader that it isn't clear who really deserves the Agra treasure as it was stolen during the rebellion known as the Indian Mutiny.
- **Interpretation**: This shows that Dr Watson is very critical of Thaddeus and very protective of Mary. Dr Watson's very negative reaction to Thaddeus's behaviour is I think used by Conan Doyle to emphasise Watson's growing feelings for Mary. The word 'wronged' shows that Thaddeus knows that they have been unfair to her and I think Conan Doyle is saying to the reader that it isn't clear who really deserves the Agra treasure.

Grade 5+ sample answer – Now you try! (page 69)

Conan Doyle also shows Thaddeus's strange reaction with 'O dear! O dear!' The use of exclamation marks here shows Thaddeus's distress and his emotional nature. This is also shown by the verbs used to describe his movements: 'jerked' and 'stamped' which creates an almost child-like image of his behaviour. Thaddeus is therefore presented as an extremely emotional character – one who is finally in a 'convulsive frenzy' where the noun 'frenzy' suggests his behaviour is almost on the verge of madness. Conan Doyle uses this as a contrast to other characters in this chapter, for example, Mary Morstan, who unlike Thaddeus is very calm and concerned about the welfare of others, and Holmes who remains controlled and unemotional.

Grade 7+ sample answer – Check the skills (page 71)

- **Points**: Thaddeus's strange behaviour is reflected in his mental and physical weakness. This is shown by his 'convulsive frenzy' which suggests uncontrolled movements almost like a medical condition. Thaddeus's generous behaviour in the novel is unusual when considered alongside the 'cursed greed' of his father and brother.
- **Context**: Thaddeus's behaviour is used by Conan Doyle as a counterpoint to that of Mary Morstan which almost reverses the Victorian stereotype of the logical male and emotional female. This use of opposite character types reflects a Victorian scientific interest in duality, such as good and evil.
- **Interpretation**: This mirrors Thaddeus's introduction in the story as a 'confirmed hypochondriac' whose main care is his own welfare. Thaddeus's behaviour, before and after the murder, is used by Conan Doyle as a counterpoint to the controlled and calm behaviour of Mary. [Thaddeus] believed Mary was a 'wronged woman' and the use of the adjective 'wronged' shows

Thaddeus's sense of justice and determination to secure Mary's rights. Conan Doyle thereby contrasts the character of Thaddeus with that of his twin.

Grade 7+ sample answer – Now you try! (page 71)

AO1
- Small's bitterness and sense of injustice are shown by the nouns used by him to describe Major Sholto after his betrayal of the Four.
- His feelings develop from bitterness to an 'obsession' with revenge.
- His thoughts turn increasingly violent and lawless showing his darker, criminal nature.
- His care for the Islander offers a counterpoint to this. Also loyalty to the Four explained in Chapter 12.
- He nursed Tonga back to health over two months, showing his better nature.
- His desire to make friends with Tonga is shown by his learning some of Tonga's language; the closeness of friendship described later in Chapter 12 as 'faithful mate'.

AO2
- The nouns 'villain' and 'scoundrel' show his bitter feelings towards Major Sholto.
- Small says his thoughts of 'vengeance' possessed him day and night.
- The imagery of violence – 'hand upon his throat' – becomes more significant and shows Small's darker character.
- Small's description of his care for Tonga over 'a couple of months' shows his kindness and his attempts to 'learn a little of his lingo' reveal a growing friendship between the two men.

AO3
- The theft of the Agra treasure during the Indian Mutiny, first by the Four and then by Major Sholto, symbolises the way in which the British took wealth from the colonies of the empire to increase their own personal fortunes.
- Small's care of and friendship with Tonga is interesting given that non-white peoples were often considered 'savage' and uncivilised by many Victorians. Conan Doyle shows Small's loyalty to Tonga which contrasts with other characters' reactions to him.

Planning your theme response – Now you try! (page 75)

- **Paragraph 1**: The extract begins with a conversation between Holmes and Watson which shows their comfortable friendship as Holmes quizzes Watson to see if he can remember details of a previous case. Watson's laughter shows he is used to this sort of test. Also similar to 'test' at the opening of the novel.
- **Paragraph 2**: The contrast between Watson's weariness and Holmes's energy is shown – 'limp', 'weary' and 'enthusiasm' – the difference between them is also the basis for their successful friendship. Also mirrors start of the novel with their different attitudes to Holmes's drug use.
- **Paragraph 3**: Watson states that he is prepared to 'devote' his life to finding the treasure for Mary even

though it would put her 'beyond his reach', showing how unselfish his love is.
- **Paragraph 4**: Holmes has cooked breakfast and clearly realises Watson is tired as he encourages him to look after himself and eat.

Grade 5 sample answer – Check the skills (page 77)

- **Points**: Conan Doyle shows Holmes earlier in the novel to be a character who does not appear to be concerned with money. Overall Bartholomew and Dr Watson are both presented here as concerned by wealth, but for different reasons.
- **Context**: In Victorian times the poor and disabled were not supported and life would have been very harsh for him without money.
- **Interpretation**: Conan Doyle suggests that Holmes is only motivated by work and this sets him apart from many of the other characters in the novel such as Bartholomew Sholto, Major Sholto and the Four who are driven by their desire for wealth. In the novel we see Jonathan Small's obsession with wealth and the treasure. First he desires wealth to improve his life because he describes himself as a 'useless cripple'.

Grade 5 sample answer – Now you try! (page 77)

In the passage Conan Doyle contrasts Major Sholto's selfish attitude to wealth with the behaviour of Dr Watson who learns of the 'gigantic sum' the treasure is valued at. His first thought is about Mary, changing her from a 'needy governess' to the 'richest heiress' and the contrast between the adjectives 'needy' and 'richest' and the low status of a 'governess' and high position of an 'heiress' shows just how significant Mary's transformation would be if the treasure were found. Watson's unselfish attitude to wealth is shown because he does congratulate her, but still has worries about his lack of money and poor health. These concerns first appeared in Chapter 2 when Watson thought that his 'weak leg' and 'weaker banking account' would create impossible barriers which would prevent his ever marrying Mary.

Grade 7+ sample answer – Check the skills (page 79)

- **Points**: Watson, however, views the treasure as a 'golden barrier' between him and Mary. Finally, although he is presented as the criminal, Jonathan Small's attitude to wealth in my view could be linked with Watson's as he also views the treasure in moral terms. In the spirit of justice and fairness he is determined that others receive their share.
- **Context**: Dr Watson's attitude reflects a rigid Victorian attitude to wealth and social class. If Mary Morstan became the 'richest heiress', then Watson, a poorly paid army doctor, would not be considered a suitable marriage partner.
- **Interpretation**: In the passage Watson says 'selfishness took me by the soul' and the religious noun 'soul' reflects his strong sense of morality regarding wealth. At the end of the novel Small says 'it's been the sign of the four with us always' and this is a symbol of his loyalty, rather than individual greed. When Small throws the treasure in the Thames it suggests that no one deserves this looted wealth and by concluding the novel with Watson's engagement, Conan Doyle emphasises the importance of love over wealth.

Grade 7+ sample answer – Now you try! (page 79)

AO1

- The relationship between Holmes and Watson is seen as a strong, familiar friendship.
- Despite their different natures, there is clearly understanding and concern for each other – shown here and elsewhere in the novel.
- Watson's growing feelings of love towards Mary Morstan are conflicted – he wants the relationship but knows that the treasure will make it impossible. His love is not selfish as he is prepared to 'devote' his life to finding it. This is echoed in Chapter 10 when he brings the treasure box to Mary to open first.

AO2

- The exchange of questions and testing of Watson by Holmes, and Watson's 'laughing' response, shows that this is a regular type of conversation between the friends.
- The contrast between the adjectives 'limp' and 'weary' and the noun 'enthusiasm' reflects the contrast between the two men. Despite this – or because of this – their friendship is strong.
- Watson is determined to find the treasure despite his fears that it will put Mary out of his reach – he dismisses regrets about the treasure as 'petty selfish love', showing how his love is selfless.
- Holmes's preparations of the breakfast and the gentle imperative 'Better have your ham and eggs' show his concern for Watson's welfare.

AO3

- Conan Doyle shows that social status and hierarchy were very important in Victorian society. If Mary had become a wealthy heiress then marriage between her and a poor 'half-pay surgeon' would be considered inappropriate.

Practice questions (pages 80–1)

Question 6

AO1

- The description of Mary at the beginning of the extract reflects Watson's romantic feelings for her and focuses on her appearance and physical beauty.
- Her response when Watson arrives with a 'bright flush of pleasure and surprise' indicates Mary's own feelings for Watson have deepened.
- Mary's response to the treasure is rather calm and cool. Her calm nature is also shown during the events at Pondicherry Lodge in Chapter 5 where she comforts the housekeeper.

AO2

- Conan Doyle uses the adjective 'white' to describe both her clothes and her skin, giving Mary a pure, angelic appearance.
- Her reaction to the treasure is understated. Conan Doyle uses the verb 'glanced' and the adverb 'coolly' which both indicate that she is not excited by the recovery of the treasure box and is therefore not motivated by wealth.
- Mary's statement that she 'owes' everything to Watson echoes her feelings of concern for him earlier in the novel where both she and Watson hold hands for a moment during the shocking events at Pondicherry Lodge.

AO3

- Conan Doyle keeps Mary away from the action of the river chase as this involves male characters only. This reflects the Victorian stereotype of men as figures of action and women as passive and emotional.
- The physical description of Mary is of an idealised beauty associated with the 'angel of the house' and the Victorian home.

Question 7

AO1

- Watson's comment which opens this extract, that the 'flying man-hunt' gave him a 'wild thrill' greater than any other chase he had experienced before, creates drama and excitement for the reader.
- Conan Doyle's constant references to distance, 'yard by yard', 'nearer … and nearer', emphasise the dramatic nature of the chase and that the police boat is gradually catching up on the criminals in the *Aurora*. A similar sense of drama is created in Chapter 7 as Holmes and Watson track the criminals from Pondicherry Lodge at night into the city of London.
- The men on the *Aurora* are not immediately identified as Small and Tonga in the passage – they are introduced simply as the 'man' and a 'huddled bundle': this creates further drama and a sense of mystery. A similar combination of drama and mystery is seen in Chapter 5 with the discovery of the murder of Bartholomew Sholto and the speculation about the cause of his death.
- Conan Doyle's animalistic description of Tonga here creates a sense of danger. This animalistic description is also significant in Chapter 12 where Small describes 'exhibiting poor Tonga at fairs'.

AO2

- Conan Doyle's use of onomatopoeic verbs such as 'panting' and 'clanking' to describe the *Aurora*'s engine plus the use of dynamic verbs 'sprang' and 'shook' to describe Small's actions dramatises events for the reader. This is similar to the night-time ride across London to Pondicherry Lodge where imagery of 'gloom' and darkness is used to heighten the tension.
- Conan Doyle's description of Tonga – first using the pronoun 'it' then using animalistic imagery with 'savage, distorted creature' – heightens the sense of danger.
- Holmes's imperative 'Fire if he raises his hand' plus the use of the adverb 'quietly' suggest Holmes is calmly preparing to shoot and therefore increases the sense of anticipation in the scene.

AO3

- Throughout the passage the river chase is described using words which echo those used in hunting, especially big-game hunting, a popular 'sport' for the Victorian ruling classes in the countries of the British Empire.
- References to the 'savage' appearance of Tonga and to his features marked with 'bestiality and cruelty' reflect Victorian attitudes to native peoples who were often characterised as uncivilised and subhuman.